Advance praise for

FOR ALL WHO HUNGER

"While church leaders were asking 'How can we get our message out into the world?,' Emily M. D. Scott went out into the world and asked 'How can I bring this back into church?' Her haunting memoir, *For All Who Hunger,* tells the story of how she created a place for those who never felt at home in church and how her unlikely congregants, in turn, helped her rediscover the heart of her own faith. This powerful and illuminating book is a must-read for those interested in how communities of faith can learn, grow, and reclaim their vital purpose."
—Jacob Slichter, author of
So You Wanna Be a Rock & Roll Star

"*For All Who Hunger* is so full of heart and wisdom, curiosity and kindness, it seems not of this world. Perhaps it isn't, and that's a very good thing. Scott envisions a radically welcoming and nurturing space of community that speaks directly to my soul. This book is sharply observed and bursting with generous portraits of real people seeking connection. It is a story and a sermon and a gift; anyone who cares about modern faith, justice, and our relationships to one another will treasure this book."
—R. Eric Thomas, author of
Here for It: Or, How to Save Your Soul in America

"Conversion—which is to say, the revelation of the whole real world with God in it—is at the heart of this honest, intelligent, and generous book. Scott is called and accompanied by the strangers she meets on so many roads. She stumbles alongside them, carrying her people's failures and fears. She wants. She burns. She hums a song and tells a story that's a promise. And as night falls, this awkward, faithful pastor invites us all in, so that one more time our eyes may be opened in the breaking of bread."
—Sara Miles, author of *Take This Bread*

"What Scott has accomplished in this book is nothing short of astounding. In an era of increasing division and existential loneliness, she manages to do the one thing Christians and seekers have been trying to do for two thousand years: She captures community. *For All Who Hunger* is raw, authentic, freshly prepared, and ready to be broken into pieces like the communion she so beautifully shares. She doesn't turn away from her own brokenness, which somehow invites us to look at our own and find the hauntingly beautiful and fearfully made that is already occurring in our midst. In a world that is constantly looking for God and meaning, Scott reminds us that it is in the sharing of that journey with one another where God shows up."
—Lenny Duncan, author of
Dear Church: A Love Letter from a Black Preacher to the Whitest Denomination in the U.S.

"As someone who planted/launched/guided-into-existence a new church when I was twenty-six (it was my second), I read *For All Who Hunger* with delight. With extraordinary courage and tenderness, Scott speaks truth about the life of a spiritual leader in these strange times, a mixture of loneliness, deep wells, non-perfection, connection, humiliation, exuberance, awkwardness, and healing. You may have no interest in religion or church or the like, but even then, the beauty and humanity of this book will make you want to read, and to read slowly, as if you're savoring a meal spiced with love."

—Brian D. McLaren, author of
The Great Spiritual Migration

"Lutheran pastor Scott asks in her exceptional debut: if you strip from church all 'the creeds and the chasubles,' what would be left? The answer, for her, became St. Lydia's Dinner Church in New York City, which she founded in 2008 as a place for queer, marginalized, artistic, nerdy, and often lonely lovers of God to gather for bread, wine, and the words of Jesus. . . . Scott's writing is leavened by a healthy dose of self-awareness, and her stories capture the humanity of her mission and community with a light sacramental touch, focusing mostly on the joy and solidarity found in the shared space."

—*Publishers Weekly* (starred review)

"In this intimate and openly heartfelt debut memoir, Scott explores the power of faith and community as strength-building resources for navigating difficult times.... She's equally relatable and forthright in exposing her own vulnerabilities and loneliness as a single woman living in the city along with her responsibilities and insecurities ministering to the needs of her congregants. Scott delivers a moving personal memoir and an accessibly reverent meditation on finding faith through unconventional acts of worship. Highly inspiring for anyone seeking solace in our modern world."

—*Kirkus Reviews* (starred review)

FOR ALL WHO HUNGER

FOR ALL WHO HUNGER

Searching for Communion
in a Shattered World

EMILY M. D. SCOTT

CONVERGENT

NEW YORK

Library of Congress Cataloging-in-Publication Data
Names: Scott, Emily M. D., author.
Title: For all who hunger / Emily M. D. Scott.
Description: First edition. | New York: Convergent, 2020.
Identifiers: LCCN 2020003072 (print) | LCCN 2020003073 (ebook) |
ISBN 9780593135570 (hardcover) | ISBN 9780593135587 (ebook)
Subjects: LCSH: Scott, Emily M. D. |
Lutheran Church—New York (State)—New York—Clergy—Biography. |
St. Lydia's (Brooklyn, New York, N.Y.) |
Church development, New—New York (State)—New York. | Brooklyn
(New York, N.Y.)—Church history. | New York (N.Y.)—Church history. |
Food—Religious aspects—Christianity. |
Dinners and dining—Religious aspects—Christianity.
Classification: LCC BX8080.S345 A3 2020 (print) |
LCC BX8080.S345 (ebook) | DDC 284.1/74723—dc23
LC record available at https://lccn.loc.gov/2020003072
LC ebook record available at https://lccn.loc.gov/2020003073

Printed in Canada

Book design by Edwin Vazquez

2 4 6 8 9 7 5 3 1

First Edition

For my parents, David and Marilynne,
who took me to church,
and for each and every Lydian,
who made one with me.

They need not go away;
you give them something to eat.

—Matthew 14:16

CONTENTS

IV. RESURRECTION

AUTHOR'S NOTE

This book is a memoir: a story made of memories. In service of the narrative, I have tinkered with time lines. To protect privacy, some names have been changed. I have endeavored to tell the truth.

FOR ALL WHO HUNGER

PROLOGUE

Communion

Well, if it's a symbol, to hell with it.
—Flannery O'Connor, on the Eucharist

In my hands I hold a warm loaf of bread. I lift it to eye
level, so it can be seen. I sing words: about how Jesus
took bread and blessed it and broke it, and as I sing, I rise
up on my toes without realizing and close my eyes. *No,
keep them open,* I remind myself, and look around the room
at the twenty-five souls gathered there.

We stand in a loose circle around three tables set for
dinner: mismatched napkins, forks and spoons, bowls
filled with a green salad. Behind me, a pot of soup steams
on the stove top. The people's hands are lifted, held open
in prayer, like mine. Some have their eyes closed, faces
tilted up in expectation. Others look back at me. The pastor has a privileged place in the gathering: we get to see
our people at prayer. Their eyes are soft, waiting to receive.

There is a tenderness to this moment, shot through with quotidian distractions. One congregant might fret about the testy arch of her supervisor's eyebrow when she asked for tomorrow off. Another prays fervently that his sister will stay clean this time, while another may just be realizing he forgot something at the grocery store. One has dredged himself from the quicksand of yet another depressive spell just to make it to church tonight. They are seeking love or sex, working two jobs to pay the rent, hungry for fulfillment, achievement, attention. I know their stories. Some grew up in poverty and others were raised to go to prep school. They dream of making it as an artist or just making it through the day.

The song leader chants and we repeat together: "Glory to you forever and ever."

It's dark outside, and in the plate-glass window of our storefront, the reflections of candles flicker as somebody races by on their bike. There's a fire station down the street; often the room floods with circling red lights and the blare of the siren.

"Mother, we give you thanks for the life and knowledge you sent us through Jesus your child," I sing before catching the eye of one of the newcomers in the room, a clean-shaven kid with a mess of curly hair and a flush to his cheeks. He can't be more than twenty-five. He has the look of a new arrival to the city, his face not yet hardened into the feigned certainty of the urban dweller. He takes in the chanting, eyebrows raised and a surprised smile on his face, like he's just woken up from a spell.

Sometimes I wonder what pedestrians think as they pass by on the sidewalk and catch a glimpse of us inside. There we are, standing in a circle, singing to bread.

I break the loaf. It's fresh from the oven and hot in my hands. When the crust cracks, steam escapes in curls, and I hear an audible sigh from the congregation. It is so good, this bread. It smells of rosemary and yeast. You feel its breaking in your bones, deep down somewhere. The warmth of it on a cold night.

"Holy food for holy people," I say, turning my gaze to the room. My people look at me, and at the bread. The eyes of the people shine. It's a moment outside of time.

I turn to Malika, a congregant standing next to me, her dark hair swept off her neck and held up with a beaded hairpiece, and tear off a piece from the loaf.

"Malika," I say, pressing the piece into her hands, "this is my body."

I meet her eyes and then avert mine quickly. These are not easy words to say. They evoke a letting go of self, the smell of sex, an errant thought of cannibalism in the back of the mind. Malika takes the bread and eats it.

"Amen," she says.

She takes the loaf from me and gives a piece to Will, standing next to her, owlish and academic in his horn-rimmed glasses.

"Will, this is my body."

The bread is passed from hand to hand. I collect the leftovers in a basket, and pop it on the table closest to me, ready to be smeared with butter or dipped in soup. Then, we all sit down to dinner.

Often, I have to explain who I am and what I do to confused men I've met online in my attempt to have something resembling a normal social life. One such date was with an avowed agnostic and medical student. We met for drinks at a sidewalk café on the West Side of Manhattan.

"So, your church, St. Lydia's . . . you eat dinner?" he asked me. He was gangly, curious, and good-natured. I already knew that I liked him.

"Well . . . we all cook and set up for dinner together," I said, abashedly. "We sing and light candles, and I bless the bread, and we share it. We eat, talk about scripture, and share our stories. And then we hold hands and pray, clean up together, get a blessing, and go home." Like a big nerd, I went on to explain that the worship at St. Lydia's is patterned after an early Church practice of sharing a common meal: in the first few centuries of Christianity, worship took place not in a sanctuary full of pews, but around a handful of tables in people's homes.

He frowned, considering my words.

"Sorry," I said, reflexively. "That's probably more information than you want."

"No, no," he responded, smiling. "That actually sounds . . . really nice. It sounds like some of the evenings I spend with good friends. When the food is good and the conversation is good. Those nights feel sacred to me."

"I agree!" I told him. "I think they're just as sacred as what I do in church on Sunday night."

This particular agnostic later broke up with me on the sidewalk in front of my apartment just after kissing me, which seemed an unusual choice of sequencing. But whenever I explain St. Lydia's, I think of him, because he saw what we were doing so clearly. Church is not about transcending human things like warm food and chortling laughter. It is—or should be—about pointing to them as sacred. Our most human parts are also the most holy.

I became a Lutheran pastor against my will. I never really meant to.

"How did you decide to become a minister?" someone asks me. My hairdresser as she captures portions of dampened hair between comb and blade; a friend of a friend at a party as she smiles and smooths her boyfriend's dress shirt; the young seminarian who looks up at me with wide open eyes, hoping to catch sight of her own illuminated future.

My heart curls inward, like a crustacean receding into its shell. It's a simple question, completely innocent, yet it seems impossible to answer.

"God made me do it" are the words that usually flash through my mind. I don't say them out loud, though. They taste too bitter in my mouth for casual conversation. Usually I smile, lips pressed together, and say something like "That's a long story," and wonder how I might manage to explain.

At gatherings of Lutheran clergy, I don't fit in. I am young, I am female, I am not married, I do not have chil-

dren. There are some younger clergy and women scattered
through our assembly, but the majority of Lutheran pastors are men who were ordained decades ago. They all
seem larger than I am, delivering strong handshakes to
one another, inquiring about wives, and cracking loud
jokes. *Har har har.* They wear their clerical collars with
ease, as if born into the uniform. With black suits and
white collars, they mingle like a colony of penguins in a
huddle.

I know a lot of these men. Many of them have welcomed and affirmed me, offering words of encouragement
and resources to share. They are kind. I like them. But
when they're all assembled together, it's clear I'm out of
place. I've wandered into the wrong zoo exhibit, a small
bird with unruly plumage. My heart starts racing beneath
my garish feathers.

St. Lydia's, the church I founded and for the last seven
years served as pastor, is a convention of odd birds. Each of
us would be wholly out of place wandering through the
doors of a clapboard, steepled church. Most of us are
younger than the average church-attending Christian by
at least twenty years. Many of us are single, many of us are
Queer. We are the kids who hung out in the art room long
after the bell rang but flunked out of algebra. Or maybe
we earned a 4.0 but carried a constant yearning for something different, something far away, which brought us to
this city of a million lights and hard realities. Our congregants are quirky and earnest, pouring themselves into
graduate school or tugging at the threads of theological
questions. They don't believe being gay is a sin anymore,

like their pastor told them when they were kids. *But what does the Bible say about it?* they want to know. Ultimately, the thing that ties us all together, I guess, is that most of us got beat up in middle school, or narrowly avoided it.

At dinner, a congregant passes me a full bowl of soup. I scan the three tables to make sure there's someone at each with enough social skills to keep the conversation going. We've had trouble with this. The most confident Dinner Church participants tend to arrive later and end up seated at the table closest to the door. Soon they'll be guffawing loudly at a joke somebody's cracked while at the table where I'm seated, near the kitchen, we sputter and lurch through small talk.

Somewhere along the line, St. Lydia's got the reputation for being a hipster church. "Oh, yeah, the cool church," people would say to my colleague, Julia, or me when they ran into us at church events. Sometimes their words carried a hint of dismissal. Perhaps they imagined that St. Lydia's was a boutique ministry geared only toward the privileged. Or that we were unwelcoming of anyone who didn't ride a fixed-gear bike or have a mustache. Julia and I always reported these stories back to one another with incredulous laughter.

"Let me assure you," we'd tell them if we got the chance, "there's nothing about it that's cool."

Sprinkled around these tables are geeks and geniuses,

fools and misfits. Some of us have done a better job than others of climbing our way into something that might be identified as "success" in work or life. And now here we are, stumbling our way through dinner conversation that is the opposite of refined or easy.

My table struggles along. There's a computer programmer visiting for the first time who blushes whenever someone makes eye contact with him. Harrison bounces around from shelter to shelter, and always has a long story to impart; two Lutheran pastors visiting from Des Moines listen, nodding. Malika sits across from me, listening with focused patience to Gerry, a retired electrician whose pants are held aloft with a set of elastic rainbow suspenders, as he describes the technical details of a recent repair. Next to me, the new computer programmer and his tablemate have lapsed into a weighted silence that seems likely never to end. They sip their soup, staring straight ahead.

Across the room at the rowdy table, Jason, an affable engineer with a head of curly hair, leans close to Ula in her wheelchair, trying to understand what she's saying. She had a stroke a few years ago and finds it hard to string words together. She is also hard of hearing, so Jason is forced to lean close to her wheelchair and yell.

"WHAT DID THE DOCTORS SAY ABOUT YOUR MAMMOGRAM?" he shouts.

The scene elicits a familiar feeling for me: 49 percent flight reflex, 51 percent tenderness. A not-insignificant portion of me wants to run out the door. But keeping me in my seat is a warm wash of love for the people in this room. My congregants are often exasperating, unbelievably generous, reliably surprising, and very dear to me. And they keep coming back to do something that isn't all that easy—make halting conversation with a stranger— because there is something at these tables that is more important than being cool.

I think often of Jonah, God's reluctant prophet who tried to run everywhere but the place he was being sent.

"Go to Nineveh," God said. It was a simple instruction, yet Jonah balked.

"Tarshish," Jonah says to himself. "I'll go there!" It's like deciding to lie low in Pittsburgh, or Boise. "Yes, that's the answer. Tarshish will be just right."

But it was not just right. God did not say Tarshish, God said Nineveh. So Jonah ends up getting dumped over the side of a ship, swallowed by a giant fish, and, eventually, spat out onto the beach, putrid and soaking. All of that before he'll agree to just go to Nineveh and speak the words God's given him. We all do our kicking and screaming.

Christians have this strange notion of a "call," which means doing things that don't sound too appealing. If God had said to me, "Movest thou unto New York City, and startest thou a Dinner Church with no funding, no training, and no paycheck," I would have started looking around for road signs to Tarshish. Generally, our call makes us want to run like hell in the opposite direction. But there's also something about these "calls" that won't let us go. Something alluring and compelling and a little intoxicating that we can't help responding to, despite our best intentions and the flutter of fear.

I need everyone together around one table. It's the only thing that makes me whole. And so, despite my trepidation, I kept taking step after step to bring a church into being.

"Why did you decide to become a pastor?" a friend of a friend, perfectly coiffed, asks as she takes a sip from her cocktail glass at a party we're both attending.

I didn't decide, I wish I could say. *It wasn't a choice.*

When it's time to preach, I stand up and ring a bell to get everyone's attention, and then invite someone to read the scripture passage for the evening. We're reading a story from the Gospel of John, about a woman who meets Jesus when she's drawing water from the well. She's the kind of person who gets talked about around town, other women casting glances and turning their heads to whisper. But she's the first person in the Gospel of John to understand who Jesus is. "He told me everything I have ever done," she tells her neighbors, astonished.

We listen to the story. There's a silence, and another congregant reads it again. Every week, I invite people to share a word or a phrase that struck them in the text.

"Mountain," Charlotte says.

"Ancestor," someone else offers.

"The well is deep."

Then I preach. The congregants turn in their seats or pivot their chairs toward me as I explain why it's so un-usual that this woman meets Jesus alone, at the well, in the middle of the day. After, we hold a silence and I invite them to share a story of their own. Angela, a jazz saxo-phonist, is thinking about the message this woman is given to share, and wonders how her work makes an impact on the world. Jake, a writer, reflects on what it feels like to be seen by someone. Ula, our most cantankerous congregant, enthroned on her wheelchair, takes issue with the way Jesus chastises this woman for having had five husbands.

"I don't like that," she tells us flatly. "Jesus is being very judgmental."

"Thank you, Ula," I say.

We hold hands and pray. People utter fragments of hopes and pain, asking God to please help their sister, give them guidance, bring peace to our world. A congregant stands up holding a poem she's chosen to accompany to-night's scripture reading. "I am water rushing to the well-head, / filling the pitcher until it spills. . . ."[1] she reads, Jane Kenyon's words opening a space to breathe. I tear up, not expecting to. I love these people. We stand, and I chant a blessing over our cups, and we drink.

Then it's time to clean up. We do this together as a congregation; it's part of the service. Julia, our staff coordi-nator, stands at the front and doles out jobs: dishwashing, wiping down tables, sweeping and mopping the floor.

"If you don't know what to do, just ask someone who looks like they know what they're doing!" she calls out, as twenty-five people, a third of them new, begin running around like ants in an anthill, ferrying bowls to the folks washing dishes, who splash sudsy water as they work. Ula swipes ineffectively at a table and inadvertently topples a bowl of soup onto the floor. Six people rush over to help clean it up. Ezra and Burke stand with mops in their hands waiting for the dishes to be cleared, talking about Kierkegaard's influence on Karl Barth. Malika is telling me the story of her latest breakup.

"Well, it just sounds like he has some deep-seated issues with commitment," I tell her, half distracted by the clean-shaven newcomer, who is hunting around for the dustpan.

"Billy," I call to him, "look behind the bathroom door!"

After cleanup, cookies are placed on the counter, and the offering plate is passed from hand to hand. Announcements: the theology circle will start meeting next week. Sign up to cook or deacon or song-lead. Attend the protest against mass incarceration with Faith in New York. And don't forget about the upcoming retreat.

We sing a hymn. It's four-part harmony and the tenors struggle but have their line solid by the third verse. I sing a blessing over the congregation, and their hands mark out the sign of the cross, tracing a line from forehead to rib cage, one shoulder to the other. We pass the peace with hugs and handshakes and greetings that spill out the door and onto the sidewalk.

I head back to the kitchen, where a few people are helping Julia with the last bits of cleanup. Standing with the fridge open, she brandishes a large Tupperware container with a minuscule amount of leftover broccoli inside.

"WHO WOULD DO THIS?" she demands, incredulously, a hand on her hip. "Just finish the broccoli!"

"It's just to get on your nerves, Julia," someone calls back at her.

Angela informs me that the doorknob to the bathroom has somehow broken during the evening. She scrawls a sign on printer paper, "PLEASE KNOCK LOCK BROKEN," and tapes it up on the door.

Something is always breaking or broken, it seems, some tiny but crucial piece of equipment that takes three trips to various hardware stores to replace. I can sit with someone whose brother has died or exegete an arcane biblical text, but am flummoxed by the broken sump pump in our basement. We have no building manager or custodian, so tonight it's Julia who sweeps and mops down the bathroom, and I pull the garbage out to the curb.

Then we are finished, and Julia locks the door to our small storefront, which sits nestled between low brick row houses. We have checked to make sure all the candles are out. Every so often I wake up at three in the morning, wondering if the candle in the bathroom is still lit and imagining the whole place ablaze, so now we triple-check. Julia and I say good night and strike out in our separate directions, she for a drink with friends, I toward home, north on Bond Street, over the ruptured sidewalks.

St. Lydia's sits a stone's throw away from the banks of a toxic canal. The waters of the Gowanus are stagnant, slick with the refuse of brass foundries and textile mills that once stood on its banks. Through the 1800s, these industrial machines poured whatever by-products they created directly into the water. In addition, a long-dead civil engineer made a string of poor decisions that eliminated any source of running water at the canal's head. And so the toxins stewed there for a hundred years, mingling with raw sewage from Brooklyn's turn-of-the-century slums. Now the Gowanus is one of the most polluted waterways in the country. We joke affectionately about it in the neighborhood; it emits a foul odor and glistens with oil. But there is a feeling of derelict shame about the place, as if the sins of our past are concentrated here, odiferous so we might not forget them.

Rising up around the canal, the neighborhood is a study in contrasts. The high-rises under construction near downtown Brooklyn and their attending cranes are universal symbols of the encroaching ultrarich. Closer to the church are the low brick towers of the Gowanus Houses, public housing units that seem eternally enshrouded in scaffolding. There, neighbors sit out on their stoops, gossiping or watching toddlers play. Heading home from Dinner Church, I pass a bus depot where an unnamed company parks their fleet off-hours. Music pulses from a trendy bar called Swan Dive, and just south of that there's an unlikely set of luxury condominiums ready to be leased, offering twenty-four-hour concierge, valet, dry cleaning, and dog-walking services. Only in Brooklyn can luxury sit so close to dereliction. Only here can you build condos on a Superfund site and call it waterfront property.

Despite the encroaching high-end rentals, the Gowanus still seems like one of the last untamed places left in the city, at least for now, in 2015. Flanked by abandoned factories and weedy lots, and spanned by a few sagging bridges, it feels like you could get lost here and never be found. A local podcaster once reported a story that involved trespassing in an empty cement factory at night; he discovered a goat running free through the building. I once observed a tiny bulldozer floating on a miniature barge in the canal, its purpose unknown. A few weeks later, it was gone. Overnight, giant graffitied murals appear on cement walls that rise directly from the canal's waters, as if the artists suspended themselves on rigging to do their work. Along the Union Street Bridge, a derelict boat floats half submerged in the water.

It's been like this for as long as anyone can remember. The Gowanus is a place for abandoned things. It's also the place where our church ended up.

"Go ye to Gowanus," the Lord said unto me, and the leviathan ascended from the virulent deep and spat me onto the banks of this canal, slick with slime and shuddering. Here I stand at the edge of the water, in the rift between excess and poverty, between the emptiness of the well fed and the yearning of all who hunger.

This is a story about how bread, broken and passed from hand to hand, rescued me from my aloneness. Perhaps you've been alone as well, and need to be reminded that, despite all evidence to the contrary, your aloneness will not last forever. When I think of what our church made together, I think of those small beacons of light reminding you that even if you haven't found it yet, there is a shore somewhere, and you won't drown in these depths.

What can a loaf of bread do? It's just bread. It can't rewind the centuries of misuse of this canal. It can't restore the estuary or bring back the oysters that once multiplied in its waters. It can't erase the history we all know but would rather not see: that the mills along this river were built by slaves. A loaf of bread can't convince the 1 percent looking down from their condo on the twenty-first floor that the Vacant signs hanging in their hearts are tied directly to the pillage of their life's work. It can't produce a job that pays more than minimum wage for the woman who turns the elderly man in his bed or rises early to scrub someone's brownstone. It can't keep the child safe as he crosses the street to the corner store to pick up milk and peanut butter, pulling up his hoodie against the wind. Bread can't bring the father back home or restore the lost child. It can't satisfy the longing for a world connected, found, or redeemed.

Or perhaps it can.

I

CREATION

The world begins at a kitchen table.
No matter what, we must eat to live.

—JOY HARJO

Womb

A memory:
    We pitched our tent close to a lake. It was August in Vermont; some friends from grad school and I had driven north to spend a summer weekend camping. One night, when the fire had burned down to embers, my friend Michael and I walked down to the water, he to smoke a cigarette and I to take a swim. Fir trees stood sentry around us in the pitch-black darkness as we made our way to the water by feel. At the shore, we gazed up to see countless stars thrown across the sky, mirrored perfectly in the water.

I took off my clothes, set them on a rock, and waded in. The water felt as warm as a bath. Step by step I moved deeper along the sandy bottom, a circle of ripples running ahead of me in the moonlight. I swam out a ways and turned to float on my back, looking up to the constellations. For someone accustomed to the constant yellow of streetlights, the stars were uncommonly bright. I began to lose track of where the sky ended and the water began.

In the beginning, when God created the heavens and the earth, the earth was a formless void and darkness covered the face of the deep . . .

In the Bible, God makes the world out of a dark water of nothingness. I imagine this formless void as a womb, but also a tomb: a cavern waiting with the possibilities of both life and death. The image reverberates for me. My great-grandmother Beatrice drowned in the water. She found her ending in the inlet that hugs the city of Vancouver, British Columbia. When she left the house that night, in despair over her husband's death, she told her grown son that she was just up to make herself a cup of tea. She waited for him to fall asleep, then walked out the door in her nightclothes, padded down the street to the pier, and walked over the edge. The choppy waters were not warm. She didn't know how to swim.

Beatrice was a bright bloom in our family, but she would float away into depression for months or years at a time. When her head sank under the waves that night, it wasn't the first time; it was just the last. Go even farther back. When she was a baby, the priest held her in his arms, scooped the water from the baptismal font, and let it trickle over her brow. "Grant that this child may die to sin and rise to newness of life," he intoned. In her long baptismal gown, she kicked her small legs, and let out a cry.

In that lake tucked in a corner of the woods in Vermont, I was held suspended in the material of the cosmos, like a child in the waters of the womb. It was time to swim to shore, but as my gaze fell from the endless stars to the dark horizon, I couldn't find the beach. The view looked the same in every direction. My awareness shifted to the water below me, which grew deeper every minute, yawning and unknowable. Images formed in my mind of the creatures that might live below. They had palpitating gills and webbed translucent fingers; at any moment they would brush by my ankles. Panic crept in. I was aware of my nakedness. I couldn't see Michael on the shore. What if I couldn't find my way back?

The beginning is a lonely place. We hang there as if strung by invisible thread, unsure which way is up or down, the stars scattered across the water above us and below. Unknown creatures glide ominously up from the deep. Yet in these beginnings God, like a star being born, compresses herself into something as fragile and earthy as you or me, or a girl named Mary, or a friend keeping watch on the shore.

From the water I saw it: the ember of his cigarette glowing hot as Michael inhaled. And I struck out from the fathomless deep, to find the place where my feet reached the sand.

I once spoke on a panel at my divinity school. Afterward, a woman approached me. She was a generation or so older—ordained when it wasn't an easy task for women. We chatted briefly. She had an openhearted, gentle look about her that made me want to listen.

"This might sound strange," she said, "but I've been following the work you're doing, and I just wanted to tell you, that I see that something is gestating in you. And I affirm what is coming into being. And," she continued, "I want you to know that I'll be part of your cloud of witnesses. I'll be praying for you."

I hugged the woman, a relative stranger, and was surprised by my own tears. Later, sitting on the quad under a maple tree, I kept turning over her word: "gestating."

No one had ever put it quite that way before, but it seemed insistently accurate. Creating something new was not a process of building or forcibly making, but of gestation. While the world was dominated by masculine notions of construction, my work was a silent, mysterious drawing together. *I knit you together in your mother's womb,* someone once said. The words echoed through history until someone else penned them on parchment in the poetry of the Psalms. The verse speaks of a God who weaves something new as cells split and divide and multiply in the dark and cavernous space inside us. Artists and writers know this place—a secret, soft cave of impulse and intuition.

St. Lydia's first service took place in the season of Advent. The word comes from the Latin *adventus,* which means "arrival," or even "ripening." The season is all about gestation. We are watching and waiting for God to be born from the watery universe of a girl named Mary.

Another memory.

I was seven or eight years old, still small enough that my feet dangled above the floor in the church pew where I sat. My parents had bundled me into the car on a cold New England night, sidewalks crusted with a season of snow, and driven me to church. It was strange to be there in the sanctuary on a weeknight instead of on Sunday morning. I understood we were there for a special service in a time called "Holy Week," when you go to church a lot before finally getting an Easter basket on Sunday.

Most Sunday mornings, our worship was mundane and comforting. The priest would stretch out his arms; I thought his chasuble made him look like a great flying bat. He would turn his face upward and break the wafer with a loud crack.

"Holy food for holy people," he'd say.

I learned to cross myself and cup my hands in front of me at the altar, expectant and waiting. I made a game of letting the wafer sit on my tongue for as long as possible before it dissolved into mush, or the fiery taste of the wine washed it away.

This night, however, the church was shadowy instead of bright. The story being told seemed like something I shouldn't be allowed to listen to—Jesus flogged and mocked and tortured—and yet there I was, listening. At the end of the service, a grown-up came and used the brass candle snuffer I'd been taught to use as an acolyte (*just let it hover—you don't have to smush it into the wax*) to put out the candles one by one. Only the service wasn't over. When all the candles were out, the ladies of the Altar Guild came and began to remove everything from the altar. The Bible was carried away and the cloths carefully folded, exposing the spindly legs of the wooden tables. Now they seemed naked, as if their table-knees might knock together.

The priest took off his embroidered chasuble, then hoisted up his white robe. He held a bucket and the palm fronds from earlier that week, when the whole congregation shouted "Hosanna." Descending to his knees with the palms in his hands, he dipped them in the water and began to wash the steps in front of the altar. The church looked bare and empty. There was only the sound of the fronds scraping against marble. The priest scrubbed and scrubbed, as if he was determined to wash away years of grime, kneeling like a peasant.

The ritual felt dark and true.

I became entranced with mystery, the strangeness of these rites we carried out: eating Jesus' body, or marking ourselves with ash. I was mesmerized by the language of symbol. The idea that there are words too deep to be spoken—messages too rich or layered or complex to simply say out loud. At home my mother read to me of Aslan, how he was slain on the stone table and how it cracked in two. Little girls like me, Lucy and Susan, came to attend to the great lion's body, unknotting the ropes around his enormous padded paws and weeping. It sounded like another story I'd heard.

Meanwhile, a certain yearning silence had taken up residence at our house on Ward Street, where a small, square, stained-glass window stood watch over the wooden staircase. My fourteen-year-old sister had left our working-class Connecticut town to live with her dad across the country in California. The grief of her absence sent us each to our own corner of the house. A square meal (meat, peas, baked potato) was still on the table every evening, and CNN still clicked on once the dishes were in the sink. We all sat around one table, yet I felt as if we were each in our own small wooden boat, drifting away from one another, on a dark sea.

Unspoken questions were tucked into bed with me between the crisp cotton sheets each night. Is there more? And what do we call it? Will Aslan come and carry me away? Will my family ever find each other again? In the dark I pulled my knees beneath my chin and imagined I was curled close into the lion's body, rising and falling on his breath, his large feline purr like a steady engine.

When I was a knock-kneed twelve-year-old, my family moved across the country to Seattle. There we attended a hulking cinder-block cathedral perched on an overhang, looming above the city. The choir wove fugal voices through the capacious sanctuary, pure and clean, the harmonies winding around each other.

Faith was about beauty; God was a presence that waited just out of sight. No one taught me that if I just prayed harder God would give me a boyfriend, or if I didn't get the role I wanted in the school play, I must have sinned. No one told me to "invite Jesus into my heart." The God I encountered in the cavern of that cathedral lay hidden and waiting in the folds of our existence, revealed in moments of unpredictable transcendence.

In the stark cathedral, I could detect God's beating heart, pulsing beneath our rituals. It was not always easy to locate. We stood and sat down again, kneeled to pray and crossed ourselves. It was rote, except for when it wasn't, moments when my breath would catch. It happened when we moved up the aisle to receive communion: a procession of mismatched saints standing around the great stone altar, our hands outstretched and waiting. It happened sometimes when we sang together from the pages of the hymnal, blue bindings loose with years of use. Once in a rare while, I looked over to see that my mother was weeping.

There was so much beauty and grace. But sometimes I felt a distance between our rituals and that beating heart of God. The acolyte master instructed us kids to light the altar candles with a military precision that made me jumpy, as if bowing on the wrong step on the way to the altar would render the Eucharist invalid. The candles, the flowers, and the communion ware had to be perfect.

Church folk can focus on ritual so much that we lose track of God. We become entranced with a palimpsest: layers upon layers of thin paper written and rewritten over centuries. We are transfixed by the scribblings of aeons of traditions; the archives of how we've always done it. Yet God's heart is alive, and therefore unpredictable, impossible to manage or constrain with writings or rules. Sometimes it frightens us, and so we try to tame God into something more manageable—something we can control.

After church on Sundays my parents and I would go out for lunch on Capitol Hill, passing street kids sitting on blankets begging for change, their crumpled paper cups set before them. The kids had coal liner smudged around their eyes, pierced faces, hair sharpened into points. Next to them lay panting pit bulls with chain collars around their necks.

At church, we had just celebrated a meal where everyone, the priest said, was welcome at the table. And now, as my parents and I sat down for lunch, kids just a little older than me were sitting hungry. Twelve-year-olds are literal creatures with noses for hypocrisy. Wouldn't Jesus have invited them in for lunch? We claimed that communion would feed the hungry, but only broke a thin wafer. What would happen, I wondered, if we actually did what we said we were doing?

My first year in New York City, I am a year out of divinity school with my first real job. All my worldly possessions have been jigsawed into a U-Haul and carted up the stairs to my minuscule studio apartment. Every outing requires I study the subway map. This is where St. Lydia's begins to thread itself into being.

There are preliminary rhythms and routines: the three-stop commute to the towering sanctuary where I work as part of a large staff, planning worship services. Rehearsals with a college friend who's asked me to write music for her dance piece. *Twin Peaks* viewing parties every Sunday night at the apartment of my high school friend Heather. Life is a rough sketch of something that might be. My friendships are just filaments. I am always the new addition to a cluster of people who already know each other. I stand, smiling blankly as they share office gossip I'm not in on. Nothing feels as if it belongs to me.

My real life takes place across the telephone lines. A few times a week there's a long phone call to Rachel in Chicago, who details the latest bitchy behavior of her art school associates and plans for her final sculpture show. Rachel and I attended college together, and later both landed at Yale Divinity School, where we were roommates for a year, tucked on the second floor of a house with a screened-in porch on Canner Street. She'd enrolled there in an effort to please her parents, studying illuminated manuscripts instead of carving linocuts herself. But her energy seemed misplaced. She was often scheming up some complicated art project, like an addict craving a fix, furtively gathering supplies in her bedroom.

Rachel possessed a disarming sincerity that converted new acquaintances into best friends in the time it took to walk from the library to the refectory. She had this voluptuous, wide smile and bright brown eyes that everyone— men, women, it didn't matter—wanted to get lost in. Her charm gave way to depth; she was a clear spring with no bottom.

She could convince me to invite everyone we knew over on a Tuesday when I had a midterm the next morning because there was a guy she liked who would probably come if we invited everyone. The next morning, hungover and scrawling out an essay on Tertullian, I wondered how I had let her talk me into it. Rachel was a little bit like a magic spell. You wanted the magic, and when it was gone, you were bereft.

Rachel never felt at home at divinity school.

"I'm an artist," she finally confessed to her parents.

"We know," they said. And off she flew to Chicago to disappear into her studio for days, carving linocuts, her thick brown hair tied back in a knot, fingers bruised with ink, no conception of time and no exegesis papers in sight.

Rachel's voice is home, familiar and true as a song, while New York is still just clatter and noises. I've also carried heartbreak to this city. Before packing my things into boxes and loading everything into a U-Haul bound for

Manhattan, I broke up with the guy I'd thought I would marry. We're still in touch. Sometimes I call him and am startled by the familiarity of his voice when he answers, as if the sound is etched in my bones.

Over the phone, I explain to Rachel that my heart is aching for him, that I feel like we might make our way back to each other when the time is right.

"Emily," she says, stopping me. "I think he's moving on."

I start taking long walks at night. Without many friends, I can't think of much else to do with myself. One hot summer Saturday evening I head down Broadway past sidewalk cafés full of people whose lives seem to brim with coherence. They laugh and lift cocktail glasses studded with mint leaves or orange peels. Sitting on the ledge of the Lincoln Center fountain, I watch the jets of water move through their cycles.

At 10:00 P.M. the doors of the opera house are pushed open, and I am engulfed in a wave of operagoers, streaming past in tuxedos and silk wraps, sparkling and festooned, discussing the evening's most impressive aria. I am twenty-seven. Other people my age are going on dates or clambering down concrete stairs to shoe-box theaters. I'm sitting self-consciously on the edge of a fountain, hoping no one notices how alone I am.

I plunge forward, trying to create a new life. I take the subway unreasonably long distances, walking past bodegas and under highway overpasses to arrive at theater performances of people I kind of knew in college. Say hi and make small talk before I disappear through the exit without saying goodbye.

Despite my early departures, I meet a decent sampling of young New Yorkers and hear about their lives and work. Inevitably, in the course of our conversations, the question comes: What do you do?

"I work at a church," I say, referring to the position that brought me to New York. This is never a pleasant moment. Admitting religious affiliation in a city as secular as New York is like confessing to a judgmental stranger you attend medieval fayres in full costume or attend square-dancing competitions on the weekend, but so much worse. It renders you hugely nerdy, entirely undatable, possibly delusional, and likely not terribly smart, all in one blow. Often my conversation partner furrows her brow and recoils. Other times, she leans in, and I know I've met a fellow delusional.

"Really?" she says, her eyebrows raised. "I feel like I've been looking for something . . ."

In a city of eight and half million people, it turns out I'm not the only one who's lonely.

While we're standing at the bar waiting to order our drinks, the young woman tells me how much she misses her church back home.

"It was pretty conservative," she says, shrugging. "But everyone knew me there. It was just nice to have a place to, you know, ask those questions. About what life means. Or think about what I'm supposed to do with my life." She reaches for her thick pile of red hair and draws it around one shoulder. "I tried a couple of churches here, but they're all so big! And so formal. Everyone's dressed up and then, well, I'm single. I don't have kids or anything. I went to coffee hour and they were really nice and said hello, but . . ."

She trails off. Then she pins her eyes on me and says, "I have faith. But I don't know where to put it in this city."

I nod. I understand.

"Maybe I could come to your church sometime," she says. But both of us know it wouldn't be quite right. The church where I work is like the ones she's tried: all gray stone and steeple and unmovable wooden doors.

This conversation keeps happening. I keep meeting people who are "looking for something." After a while, I find I am carrying another question with me: What would a church for these people look like?

It felt like I couldn't get my foot in the door, many of them say. And I know it's not just a social dynamic they're talking about, but something bigger that they can't quite name. The thing they are hungry for—a place to be known, a place to be still in the face of the mystery and confusion of life, that thing that draws them to sit in the back pew of a great stone cathedral on a Sunday morning when they might have been at brunch with friends—too often it seems tertiary at any church they might attend. There, God feels like a distant ruler they've already managed to disappoint. In these moments, I think of those thin, papery layers I detected when I was a child in church. These people are yearning for a beating heart, and can't find it. What would it mean to drop the creeds and the chasubles and see what was left? Bread, wine, the words of Jesus. A table. Water for baptism and oil for anointing. What would happen if we stripped it all away?

That question lives just below my rib cage, tucked in the hollow where, I'd learned as a brass player, my diaphragm is located. There it gestates. In my fancy church office five floors up from the street, I pick up the phone and forget who it is I'm dialing. Each day I come to work and plan the worship that takes place beneath the flying buttresses of that sanctuary. I click down in my heels and rope off pews, checking that the microphones will be in the right locations. I organize the worship of God for the eight hundred souls who file in on Sunday, but it's feeling more and more like a production for broadcast instead of a service of worship.

Meanwhile the hulking church is roiling with conflict. Learning to navigate the politics is like playing Operation, that game I played as a kid. One bad move and everybody's hollering, their noses lighting up red. Motivated congregants bring fresh ideas for growth or justice work to a committee, only to be told, "Oh, that will step on the membership committee's toes" or "We couldn't possibly find the budget." After a few shots, they lose momentum and leave dejected. I hear similar stories from my fellow divinity school graduates at their first posts, of meetings rife with roadblocks and passive aggression. Sitting in a meeting as we squabble about money or field a litany of complaints about a recent typo in the bulletin, I imagine Jesus sitting in one of the wheeled chairs at the conference table, watching us with his eyebrows raised. He isn't pleased.

I'm imagining a community where no conference tables are necessary. Something that feels warm and intimate. Everyone will wear a name tag because we all feel nameless in this city, shuffling down the stairs through the turnstiles to the subway to be carried along below the teeming streets. In a place where hardly anyone has room in their cramped apartment for a dining table, cooking and eating together feels particularly potent. It could be simple but hearty—soup and bread instead of a thin wafer—recalling the practices of early Christians, whose celebrations of the Eucharist took place at the table, over a full meal.* The food will be warm, the singing simple, the prayers from the heart. No one will leave hungry.

The Question begins to demand more room.

On a brisk April evening, I meet Rachel at Grand Central Terminal amid a swirl of commuters charging home. She's flown east for the baby shower of a friend in New Haven. Together, we board the train and find a pair of red and blue pleather seats where we can sit facing each other.

By the time we reach Bridgeport I am telling her about the Question and its secret growth. Rachel is no stranger

---

*As documented by historians and evidenced by an early Christian instruction manual called "The Didache," Eucharistic celebrations in the early Church took the form of a shared meal, often hosted by a wealthy Christian.

to invasive ideas; she listens with a pointed focus. I tell her I want to build a congregation for people like her and me—people who don't find a place so easily in church but are looking for God, nonetheless: in the way the shavings fall with grace to the floor from the wood as it's carved, or in the catch of a breath between tumbling chromatics of Stravinsky.

Together on the train, we start crosshatching ideas, the cadence of our words picking up in excitement. Is it possible to create a church that's made of real life? Where people eat together around a table and sing, and where we invite the questions that have seemed muted at every church we've ever attended? I tell her I want people to feel like it's okay to swear. There will be no "church version" of ourselves, she offers, scrubbed down and shined up to cover the mess. We'll come because God will be revealed in us. In our swearing, bawdy, actual selves who make crude jokes or sometimes get a little too drunk. There will be bread and wine and the mystery that we've encountered in our art and long to encounter with a community of friends. I want to name it after Lydia, a woman in the Book of Acts. When she's remembered at all, Lydia is remembered for her hospitality, hosting the apostles. Reading between the lines of biblical text, we catch sight of an uncommon woman. She's a merchant who sells expensive purple cloth, often worn by royalty, heading her own business and her own household, no husband in sight. After her conversion, she is a founding leader of the church in Philippi.[1] Could our church be as powerful, inviting, and unflinching as she was?

And on that train steadily moving north along the cold shore Rachel says yes: if you do this, I will come and help you.

If you have ever found yourself sketching something that does not yet exist on a napkin as you wait for a friend to arrive at the corner bar, you could be in trouble. Something is happening that you are no longer in charge of.

When you begin to speak to your friends about this idea, to outline with qualifying language—"I've been wondering about" or "It might look like . . ."—and test them for signs of affirmation, you may be experiencing something resembling a call. When words feel too pale and insufficient for what you are trying to describe, but a few fellow dreamers can catch sight of it, their eyes narrowing in discovery and their lips curving into smiles, you are in very deep trouble. You have caught a kind of fever, and your life will likely change in unexpected, delightful, and troublesome ways.

I talked to everyone I knew. I called my mentor, Donald, in San Francisco and asked for materials for a dinner liturgy they used to have at his church called the "Feast of Friends." The idea gathered form and shape, became a "something" from nothing. Invisible bits of life drawn from the air, like a starter gathering yeast, and it was there. Suspended in the darkness, taking on shape and form.

There's a name for this stage, though I didn't know it at

the time. Kyna Leski, a researcher at MIT, calls it "gathering."[2] It's a precreative time of drawing together, sketching and researching and pinning scraps on bulletin boards. It involves going down a lot of rabbit holes and obsessing about ideas that eventually end up on the cutting-room floor. It's part of the process, as they say. For us, this gathering stage, this germination, lasted the proverbial nine months.

The idea was to let the symbols speak for themselves. The bread, the wine, the table. The oil and the water. To create a place where their meaning was so transparent that no one would ever say, "It's lovely, but what does it mean?"

It never would have happened if I wasn't aching with loneliness. If I had been clacking along a more familiar track of dinner and drinks, a ring of friends around me, secure in my own place in the world and headed toward an identifiable destination, St. Lydia's might never have been. My barely repressed need for connection was the very thing that allowed me to see so clearly the longings of others.

In a city of glimmering lights and cracked sidewalks, every soul, whoever they may be, in an unguarded moment when their children are sleeping in bed, or when they hear the subway rumble deep underground, or when they catch sight of the skyline pink and flushed at twilight, will allow the brusque manner or affected laugh to slip away from their shielded hearts and remember, as if in a dream, that there is something they are searching for that they have not yet found.

They know that the rope has frayed and snapped, and

that they, just like me, are in their own small wooden boats, lost on the sea.

I couldn't bear to feel like we were drifting away from each other, carried apart on the deep. So I set tables, hoping we could all find our way home.

QUICKENING

Heather ran up a table runner on her sewing machine. A friend from high school whose dark hair was often streaked with electric blue or pink, she carved a potato stamp with the logo Rachel had designed for us, then printed it neatly on each end of the runner. A square with a semicircle positioned at each side, the logo could have been a cross, or four chairs at a table. Now we were ready for church.

St. Lydia's met for the first time in the apartment of my friend Daniel, an Episcopal priest who mentored me during a summer internship in California. He did a stint as a monk, but God had something slightly different in mind. Daniel kicked up his heels, moved to San Francisco, and married an unfairly handsome actor named Javier. He still had a monkish way about him—wise, glimmering eyes framed by smile lines, and the kind of steady presence you'd expect from someone who spent a decade at prayer. He could have stood in for a Jedi in one of the *Star Wars* movies. When I told him about this church we wanted to create, he said that when he and Javier moved to Lower Manhattan that winter, he would host in his apartment and preside. He was the only person I knew with a place big enough to hold twelve people.

By strange circumstance, Daniel lived in the same building as Heather, so she threw together a winter vegetarian stew in her apartment, carried it onto the elevator with pot holders, and knocked on her new neighbor's door for the first time. Inside, we smoothed her freshly stamped runner across Daniel's table, right in the middle of the moving boxes, and began to welcome people as they arrived. There was Jake, a friend from San Francisco and incognito rock drummer; a colleague from divinity school; a church musician; and a choreographer I wrote music for. It was an eclectic group, brimming with enthusiasm. The twelve of us crowded around Daniel's modest table, our elbows bumping.

"Looks like we need a larger table," Jake said, grinning as he pulled his chair up to a corner. I was thrilled. On our first gathering, we were already out of space, and Jake seemed to be implying we should do this again!

Those first services felt like workshops. Privately, we rehearsed for what would come next, sketching the shape and smoothing the liturgy. The first night, sitting at the table and listening to Heather quiz Daniel on life in a monastery, I felt my heart glow like embers. There we were, gathered together in a city where no one's supposed to know their neighbors.

That night I read the story of the child knit together in the womb of a girl called Mary. It was four weeks before Christmas. A time of preparation for God to be born among us, known to Christians as the season of Advent. Around Daniel's table, we met for the first time as a church and waited for the whole cosmos to shift.

What do you do when you have a church but no building? The four services at Daniel's apartment have gone well—there's energy and excitement for more. But as Jake said, we've already outgrown our table. I start wandering the city, unsure what I'm looking for, but led forward by a whiff of possibility. I'm searching for some magical thing . . . a place that will house our brand-new church in a city where monthly rent exceeds the total balance of my retirement account.

There is a feeling of delight and magnetic intuition. I peer into empty storefronts hung with crooked For Rent signs, imagining our crew cooking a warm meal in the deserted restaurant kitchen. Every empty building pulses with what might be. There are no budgets yet, no price tags, time lines, or schedules—just pure dreams unfettered by reality.

Conversations with friends and colleagues lead me to

meetings with a bizarre assortment of people. Someone connects me with a wealthy Episcopalian who lives in a neighborhood I didn't even know existed. The street seems to hang suspended over the East River, gray row houses squatting heavily together like overweight pigeons on a wire. I am buzzed up to a labyrinthine apartment, all brassy fixtures polished to a gleam, where I perch on a floral settee and tell the gentleman of the house about my idea for St. Lydia's.

"Well, you'd certainly have room in here," he comments mildly, gesturing to the dining room behind him. The sturdy oak table is about a mile long; china stands at attention behind glass. Somehow it doesn't seem quite the setting. Dinner Church should be humble—accessible to teenagers begging for change and their dogs too. I didn't want anyone to wonder which fork they should use.

I poke my head into church buildings as well. Some towering structures make me feel cold inside, others draw me toward them. It's pleasurable, existing in this place of sheer possibility. Nothing's pinned down or entirely real. St. Lydia's is unformed and ephemeral, and so it has the liberty of being perfect.

Jake wonders if the Lower East Side might be a good neighborhood, so, one bright December Saturday, I ride the F train to the Broadway-Lafayette station. Aboveground, I drift among the tenement buildings. They lean under their own weight, their facades zigzagged by fire escapes, their stoops worn uneven under the shoes of last century's immigrants and seamstresses or this century's socialites and trust-fund babies. Farther north, in Alphabet City, tiny record shops are stuffed in basement-level storefronts, the splatter of jazz spilling out into the street. In Tompkins Square Park, guys thunder by on skateboards, boom boxes blaring, while a dime bag passes from hand to hand on the corner.

On Avenue B and Ninth Street, I pass a modest brick building with a small garden, its borders defined by a neat iron fence. Inside, plants grow in tidy rows, and homeless men sprawl on the steps, eating chili from paper bowls.

The garden belongs to a church, though the building doesn't look like one. There is no steeple, no big steps or giant door. Just a three-story structure nestled behind this gated garden, and a cherry tree bowing its branches toward simple stained-glass windows on the second floor. *That little church looks like they're up to something,* I think. I like how the men on the steps look at ease: as if they finally have a moment to breathe in a city that never tires of telling them to move along.

Peering around the corner, I see a line for the soup kitchen spilling out the modest door and down the wheelchair ramp. I say hello to the gentlemen waiting with their carts and bags, and make my way up to the door. There stands a solid woman whose name, I will later learn, is Lupita.

"Hi!" I call to her over the heads in line. "Is this a church?"

"Yes, it's a church!" she shouts, scowling at her clipboard and making furious marks in ballpoint pen. The men file past her into a community room where there's a buffet line.

"Would it be okay if I looked at the sanctuary?" I ask her.

"Yeah, okay," she shouts without looking up and waves me inside.

The church's first floor is dedicated to feeding people, while the sanctuary is tucked upstairs. It's quite an architectural statement, placing your ministry to the hungry on the first floor. I dodge the line and climb the staircase, passing through a set of double doors and into a modest square room. Simple cushioned chairs face a communion table. Behind it, tall windows usher in the winter light.

I can see it immediately. The chairs will be stacked to one side. Four circular tables will be spread with cloths and food. Congregants laughing and talking and sharing a meal in this small and holy space. I don't stay long. But I can see it.

The next week I swallow my fear of phone calls and dial the number listed on Trinity Lower East Side's website. To my chagrin, the pastor actually picks up the phone. I was hoping I could just leave a message.

"Trinity Lower East Side, this is Pastor Phil," he says.

"Ummm, hi, this is Emily Scott?" I fumble. I lurch my way through an explanation—that I'm working on starting a new church community that will share a meal and would the church be open to renting space to us?

"Why don't you send me a proposal?" he says. He spells out his email address. Two weeks later, Rachel and I are sitting on the futon in his office.

Pastor Phil listens intently to us, his fingers interlaced in his lap. He sits across from us in a big, lumpy armchair, wearing a crisp printed dress shirt and a gray cabled cardigan that looks so soft I have to restrain myself from reaching out to touch it. He's a lean man, with close-cropped salt-and-pepper hair and a goatee. His green eyes are kind but inscrutable. It's hard to read him. The office, I notice, feels a bit like the neighborhood: scruffy and a little threadbare from use and love. There is nothing shiny or polished here.

"So we would have worship like the first Christians did," I tell him, rattling on about isolation in the city, about how so many young people feel alienated from the church. He seems like someone who would understand, this pastor who sits in a scuffed-up office while the smells of chili and homeless people waft up from downstairs, but I am nervous. I hope I'm not insulting the church he's devoted his life to, or rubbing him the wrong way. He fixes those green eyes on me with an intimidating intensity as we spill out our vision. Rachel flashes her big smile.

In that moment, I don't know that Pastor Phil grew up, and then served, in a more conservative branch of the Lutheran tradition before he found his way to a more affirming denomination. I don't know that when he came out, he lost the faith of his childhood, his colleagues, and his friends. I know nothing of the pain he's shouldered, simply to be who he is. All I know is that he seems legitimate: a real pastor with a real collar and a real office. And I feel like the opposite of that—some young, unordained woman who thinks she can start a church.

Rachel and I finally run out of words and lapse into silence. The angle of the futon tilts back a bit, so we're forced to either sit forward awkwardly on the edge, or lean back so our feet don't quite touch the floor, as if we're two little kids.

Pastor Phil shakes his head and closes his eyes for a moment, thinking. Then he pins his green-eyed gaze on us.

"I think it's *wonderful,*" he says, delivering each word as if it were a precious artifact. "The church has failed to provide a place for so many people, and I think that something like this, something that's *different,* something that feels *alive,* something that's less *formal,* is exactly what people are looking for. And I think that Trinity should absolutely support this in any way we can."

Rachel and I look at each other, astonished. Pastor Phil gets it. We don't have to do gymnastics to explain. He just understands.

"I think you should start worshipping here in the spring," Pastor Phil tells us, "and I'm going to encourage the Church Council to not accept any rent at all. We should be supporting this kind of project. As a ministry!"

A few weeks later I'm meeting with Pastor Phil and the chair of the Church Council. I'm surprised to walk into the office and see a woman not too much older than I am: a PhD student who seems just as positive about our project as Pastor Phil is. The two of them start talking about how they could rearrange the furniture in the back office to make room for a desk for us.

That's how things will always be with Trinity. Whenever my heart clenches, expecting churchy, bureaucratic red tape or fussing from the Church Council about budget or building use, instead there are people who only seem interested in saying yes. Trinity doesn't have money to spare. But they feed everyone who walks in their door—two hundred people a day—and scoot around their furniture to make room for a brand-new Dinner Church.

Soon there's a desk in the corner of the office, wedged between the wall and the photocopier. Rachel and I walk to the Staples down the street and choose ninety-eight dollars' worth of office supplies—our first purchase from a nonexistent budget—with trepidation. Trinity doesn't have Wi-Fi yet, but there's a single ethernet cord we can use. Every Wednesday we have "staff meetings," working side by side, passing the ethernet cord back and forth between us like a hookah, depending on who needs to be online.

In pregnancy, there's a magic moment called "quickening." It's the first time you feel movement in the uterus—a flutter like a butterfly that lets you know life has drawn together. For months, cells have been growing and dividing, but now it's clear: something new is here.

St. Lydia's was quickening—we were coming into being. But *our* quickening required people: friends and mentors, gathered around this dream. Each member of this scrappy community brought something to share.

Heather with her table runner. Daniel with his prayers and his apartment. Rachel with her vision. Pastor Phil and his church with their open doors.

It strikes me that the people who crowded around to help midwife St. Lydia's into being all had something in common. Each had the gift of seeing something that was coming, but had not yet arrived. Rachel could take a scrap of possibility—the rope that hung limp from a bucket—and notice that it was beautiful. Pastor Phil had the same gift, only he saw possibility in people. He was the kind of pastor who saw something true about you before you could see it yourself. "You are a preacher and a pastor," he would tell me, pinning me with those piercing eyes, long before I could see it.

This capacity—in an artist, a pastor, a parent, a prophet—is deeply tied to the work of God. In the season of Advent, we wait on a God who breaks into a world chained by brutality and fear. We know that the world around us is crumbled, aching, and yet some of us have eyes to see what might be, and give that possibility a name. Some of us have hands that can usher God's world into this one, bringing light and hope. Love is birthed in a darkened world; she takes a first wrenching breath, and cries. This, we call incarnation.

Pastor Phil became my mentor, and Trinity the congregation that eventually sponsored me for ordination. By this time, I had left my job at the big church with flying buttresses and started teaching children's choir part-time, so I could build St. Lydia's on the side. I worked most Sunday mornings, kneeling on the carpet with my kids to drum out a rhythm pattern. Every once in a while, though, I had the chance to worship at Trinity.

Looking out over drug deals and dog parades in Tompkins Square Park, the upstairs sanctuary would fill with the most unpredictable group of New Yorkers I'd ever seen assembled in one place. There were German grandmothers fanning themselves, sitting so solidly in their chairs they seemed likely never to move again. There was an older gentleman who wore three-piece suits in solid, primary colors and a wig with curly black hair, always slightly askew. There was a gaggle of gay musical theater boys who sang in the choir. The pianist, a young man who rarely made eye contact, had been discovered by Pastor Phil via Craigslist. He played with his right foot crossed over his knee, embellishing hymns from the Lutheran canon with a gusto the likes of which no Lutheran had ever heard.

This wild assortment of people stood and sang together each Sunday morning. "Kyrie, eleison," they exclaimed in a variety of keys. "On our world and on our way! Kyrie eleison, every day!" They were an unlikely "we," drawn together to glimpse the living heart that lay beneath their ordinary lives, which ground and ached along. Their worship was not a production, but an exultation.

One Sunday, the man who wore the bright suits offered to sing a solo. He stood in front of the congregation, struggling to find his place and his note. Everyone sat, listening, eyes encouraging and hopeful. He faltered, and I heard Pastor Phil, still seated in his chair, quietly sing the melody from behind him. The gentleman's voice met Phil's, and together they found the melody. Then Pastor Phil dropped out, and the man continued on his own.

I had thought St. Lydia's, in its pre-formed state of pure imagination, had the liberty of being perfect, but I was wrong. It had the liberty of being a fantasy. Perfection, I would come to see, came with the particularity of the real—with the love that is practiced among those who are broken. The pianist's fingers ran up the keyboard and tumbled back down, and fireworks seemed to ricochet in my heart. "That we may live out your impassioned response to the hungry and the poor," the congregation sang. And I could tell that they meant it.

FEAR AND TREMBLING

Seven minutes to seven, and I stand just inside the front door of Trinity Lower East Side, like a rabbit ready to bolt. It's Sunday night, and the only people who have arrived for Dinner Church are Rachel, Heather, and Jake. Rachel gets paid to be here, Heather is the cook, and Jake signed up to be the worship leader. If no one else shows up, we'll hold Dinner Church for just ourselves. I check my phone again. Six minutes to seven.

The part no one ever talks about is the humiliation. It's humiliating to try to start a church in an aggressively secular city. To invite people to come to worship when they'll likely think you're unforgivably naïve, unsophisticated, uneducated, and conservative to believe in something so off-trend as God. It required divesting myself of the notion that I would ever, ever be anything resembling cool. I'd known this already, ever since I told my fourth-grade classmates about the performance of the Tokyo String Quartet I'd attended with my parents, and observed their reactions. But starting a church was more recent, damning evidence.

My friend Nadia, another founding pastor, told me that planting a church is a little like throwing your own birthday party every week. I found it an apt comparison. The experience seems directly correlated with that ancient reptilian metric that lives in the recesses of our minds, left over from the days of being chosen last for dodgeball teams or school dances. *Does anyone like me?* Standing at Trinity's front door, the question hangs like a deadweight I can't push aside.

After the trial runs at Daniel's apartment, we did a six-week run at Trinity Lower East Side with the encouragement of Pastor Phil. We had fifteen or sixteen people showing up. The plan was to worship once a month through the summer, then launch weekly services in September.

In those glorious days, golden and shimmering in my memory, people wrote their names on the sign-up sheet to cook dinner. Sunday afternoon I'd receive texts from them: "See you at Dinner Church tonight!" The buzz of my phone was like a hit of nitrous oxide or the feeling of a first kiss. In the evenings, congregants arrived with bunches of flowers or homemade desserts, covered in tinfoil.

Now it's the end of October, and the sheen has worn off. People have stopped texting beforehand. I have no idea who will show up or how many; each service feels like a crapshoot. Attendance drops to twelve, then ten.

We've launched too soon. That much feels obvious. But tonight is a new low, a reverse version of serendipity in which every person who's ever come to worship picked the same weekend to go out of town. Heather has cooked food for twenty, and a huge pot of curried chickpeas with spinach sits waiting in the kitchen. Jake, our former rock drummer, peruses the worship script with more care than the task merits, as if it's a Philip Glass score. It's just the three of us until Pastor Phil and Joey come down from the rectory upstairs. Then, at five past seven, as I chatter nervously, a single newcomer arrives, a young woman with cropped blond hair bearing a package of Milano cookies. We all fall over ourselves to greet her in a high-pitched welcome.

"YOU BROUGHT COOKIES!" I exclaim, startling her. She actually takes a step back from me. "THANK YOU SO MUCH—THIS IS AMAZING!"

During worship we ladle out bowls of Heather's curry, carrying on energetic conversation with the overwhelmed newcomer, while I silently perish from mortification.

Her name is Charlotte, we learn. Fresh out of the Peace Corps, she spent the last two years in Mozambique and moved to New York just a few months ago. Reeling with culture shock and searching spiritually, she's lonely for the close community she found in the Peace Corps and sifting through her feelings about religion. Charlotte doesn't seem as traumatized by the evening's turnout as I am.

"This is wild!" she says as Rachel shows her where to stack the bread baskets in our storage closet. "I can just arrive in New York and sit down for a meal with a whole bunch of people? And on my first night, I know where the bread baskets go!"

I'm heartened by Charlotte's response. But the mortification remains.

"How you doing?" Jake asks, encouragingly, as we carry tables back to the community room together.

My family connection to Jake goes way back—he knew me when I was in the sixth grade. He's a decade older than me and a head taller, so he feels kind of like a big brother. Jake had a whole career playing drums for a successful band, a former life he rarely alludes to. Now he's a writer, wry and whip smart. He's lanky and long-legged, with a slightly haunted look he counterbalances with a broad, enthusiastic smile. I think he's sensed that I'm chagrined.

"Jake," I tell him. "Seven people. *Seven* people."

"Well," he says, lifting his shoulders in a shrug. "That's seven people who aren't in the self-help aisle at Barnes and Noble." I crack a smile, rolling my eyes while he continues. "Seven people who were here instead of eating a TV dinner."

We pop the legs of the table open and swing it upright. I laugh.

"That's true."

A few years later, with St. Lydia's safely up and running, I attended a training session for "mission developers"—people who start new churches. I remember talking with one church planter in an elevator. After listening to a day's worth of presentations about holding one-on-ones and tracking metrics and launch events and blah blah blah, he left the room convinced that his church was failing.

"We're not growing," he told me mournfully. "People come to stuff but nothing seems to go anywhere."

"How far in are you?" I asked him.

"Six months."

"Are there always like eight people at everything?"

"Yeah."

"Does it feel like sand slipping through your fingers? Like something's almost happening but it won't quite take off?"

"Yeah," he answered.

"That's totally normal. That's what it felt like for us at six months. Just keep going. It will shift."

This was basically the advice I received from my own mentor, Donald, who had started a church as well. I called him monthly, spilling stories that I was sure were indicative of our approaching demise.

"Yes, that happened to us too," Donald would say. "I remember that phase. I wouldn't worry about it. It will sort itself out in a few months." Donald would tell me a story about how St. Gregory's learned together, becoming a community that could take on challenge and conflict. At St. Lydia's we could barely manage cleanup. I struggled to trust his words, even as they offered me hope. I was like a church-plant hypochondriac, certain that there was something wrong with us, and whatever our diagnosis, it was sure to be fatal.

Church planting is a lot like child rearing. Both make you feel as if you must be ruining the life of this small being you're trying to raise toward adulthood. Both force you to reckon with elements of your own personality you'd rather not face. Both send you running to someone who's done this before you, asking if you've fouled it all up. The answer, usually: "It will be fine."

I'm certain that I projected all kinds of crap on my church-plant baby. I set St. Lydia's up with issues they'll need to work through with a therapist when they reach midlife. We all mess our kids up. The mess, however, is rife with possibility—containing the promise of strength and gift.

That fall, I build a thick skin for awkwardness. Every week I lead us in song and prayer, even when there are just four or five in attendance. "We're building St. Lydia's together," I say hopefully, "and we're still kind of figuring it out." Saying it out loud reminds me that it's true.

While the first half hour feels excruciating at times, something always seems to shift over the course of the night. We take hands and pray; I feel my breathing slow and my chest unclench. The room seems wider. Rachel stands up and reads a poem with tenderness and intellect. The words vibrate with truth, and unknot something in my gut that needs to be unknotted. We sing a hymn, and my heart feels like it's blossoming, even when the melody falters. Even on the worst-attended evenings, God shows up in an empty seat and prays with us.

After worship we clean up together in a riot of energy. We have a habit of breaking things. Heather slams the handle of the mop into a clock that hangs over the kitchen door while enthusiastically swabbing down the kitchen. A visiting priest from Oakland drops the vase from behind the altar while attempting to dispose of last week's withering chrysanthemums. It seems like every week I write another apologetic email to Pastor Phil, explaining the latest casualty and promising to purchase a replacement.

By the end of the evening I am always exuberant and joyful, washing dishes in a cascade of laughter and soapsuds. We go home better for having come.

Soon, our numbers start to build. New congregants show up with these looks on their faces, as if trying to decide whether this is a real thing, and if they want to hang around for it to get realer. Worship begins with cooking and setup. As they arrive, Rachel sends people off to chop salad ingredients or set out napkins and silverware. Everyone gets a job. The people who love the idea of making something new are the ones who stick around. Them, and people who need more love than the world is able to give them.

We meet Raphael, an East Village character with a leather cap and a pronounced limp, who leans heavily on his cane and invites us to the Christmas Day barbecue for the homeless he cooks every year in the community garden down the street. There's a huge ex-member of a motorcycle gang with face tattoos. There's Mina, a frail, birdlike girl who says very little, but tells me she's sleeping on the couch of someone she barely knows. There's Jebediah, who conducts himself with a level of dignity and decorum suitable to meeting the queen, but who is likely homeless. He contributes erudite comments after the sermon and leaves as soon as there's a moment to slip out the door without saying goodbye. These, plus people who are young and often new to the city. Charlotte, the newcomer with cookies I accosted, miraculously comes back the next week and signs up to lead worship.

Then, Ula arrives. I know Ula from my days at the big Manhattan church. She's a cantankerous presence who leans on a cane and lugs a cacophony of overflowing tote bags wherever she goes. She's always digging through them for some object that's fallen to the bottom, spilling refuse around her. With a halo of dark, untamed hair, she's known by just about every clergyperson in Manhattan. Ula attends Riverside's morning service and St. Bart's in the evening. She goes to Wednesday services at St. Michael's and Bible study at Grace Church. Everywhere she goes she demands attention. She asks agitating questions at inopportune times during annual meetings, quibbles with the pastors' interpretations of scripture at Bible study, complains to the ushers about the language in the prayers.

When I see Ula appear on the corner of Avenue B and Ninth Street, aiming straight for our door, I take a deep breath. Ula installs herself at St. Lydia's, and has plenty of opinions to share. She complains about the food, interrupts Heather as she shares a reflection, then falls asleep at the table. She always finds something to take issue with, and comes armed with comments that seem designed to make me feel small.

I worry that her quarrelsome nature will put a damper on our dinner congregation. But Heather and a few other extroverted congregants prove capable of keeping a conversation going with the most unlikely assortment of people. When my dreaded archnemesis Awkwardness shows up, I learn to invoke Julian of Norwich, repeating, "All shall be well," in my mind. Soon I can trust that, despite our patchy conversation and thin singing, we will make it through to the prayers, and at some point that evening the needle will find the groove. A tender story told at the sermon sharing, the weightlessness of silence, and suddenly, there's music.

Our church weathers its nadir, but riding our swell of energy into the spring gives me reason to be fearful about something else. On the first warm day of the year, I walk south on Sixth Avenue to meet my friend Mieke at the Cornelia Street Café. Weaving through the maze of cobblestone streets, I dodge a typical cast of West Village characters: a rail-thin model carrying two teacup Chihuahuas in her purse, all three wearing sunglasses; bodega owners out sweeping the sidewalk; a line cook smoking a cigarette on the stoop, head thrown back in a laugh as he shoots the shit with a couple of regulars.

Mieke is a pastor—a Presbyterian, and one of the first out lesbians ordained in the denomination. Colleague after colleague kept insisting we would love each other, so finally one of us wrote the other an email. We met up for dinner and talked for three and a half hours.

Like me, Mieke's single, and, like me, she has an array of alarming stories about the harsh realities of dating in New York. We trade them like baseball cards, calling each other in the middle of the workday to report the most recent travesty. The executive director of a scrappy organization fighting for LGBTQ inclusion in the Presbyterian Church, she is hilariously candid and always has a blunt opinion to offer. She sits across from me, wrapped in a woven shawl, fine nutmeg hair tucked behind her ears, scowling as she listens to my most recent dating disaster.

"So I've been on OkCupid, you know?" I report. She nods. "And there was this guy who was writing me, and he asked what I did. And I was so tired of hedging around about it that I just said, 'I'm starting a church,' and I sent him the link to St. Lydia's—which I know probably wasn't smart but I'm just so tired of it."

"Uh-huh," she responds, spearing her mixed greens furiously with her fork, anticipating the coming affront to womankind.

"Anyway then the next week at church this guy shows

up, and I thought he seemed familiar but he wouldn't really tell me how he found out about St. Lydia's . . ."

"OH MY GOD." Mieke slams the fork down and rolls her eyes. "It was him."

"It was HIM! But he didn't TELL me it was him! I figured it out right before I preached! And then I had to hold hands with him during the prayers and it was SO WEIRD. Then he darted away at the end after being totally cryptic."

I sit, chagrined.

Mieke rolls her eyes up and lets out an extended sigh. "Well? Does he want to date you?" she asks.

"Probably not after he listened to me talk about Jesus all night."

"Why did he come there?" she demands.

"He said he's been looking for a church and also someone to date, so he thought maybe he could find them both in one place. Like one-stop shopping?"

"It doesn't *work* like that," Mieke erupts. "You're at *work*! You can't be his pastor and also date him!"

"I mean, I know that. But they don't really know that."

"Would I ever show up at your job if you were . . . an accountant or something?" Mieke questions me, plowing back into her salad. "It's so weird."

"The thing is," I tell her, "he's the only one who wrote me back. Everybody else just stops writing when I tell them what I do. It's like being a pastor neuters me or something. Makes me immediately not sexy. I went out with this one guy who just wanted me to apologize for all the sins of Christendom. I get it . . . we get a lot wrong as a religion. But that's a lot for a first date."

Mieke looks at me sympathetically. "It's not easy," she says. "You're sure you're not a lesbian?"

I consider a moment, thinking about boobs.

"I . . . can't quite get there."

She nods, accepting my shortcomings.

"Pastor Phil is really encouraging me to go forward for ordination," I tell her. "I just . . ."

"You're afraid you'll never get married if you get ordained."

"Yeah. Is that crazy?"

"Based on the evidence, it doesn't seem crazy."

"I want both," I tell her.

"Me too," she says, shaking her head helplessly. "Here's to pastor life," she offers.

Under the red-striped awning, we clink our mimosa glasses, and toast our solitary futures.

One night that spring, our church reaches an important milestone. At the end of worship, the floors freshly mopped and smelling of cleaning solvent, Charlotte says, "Hey, does anyone want to get a drink?"

I've been waiting for someone else to suggest it. *Here they are,* I think, *not just coming to church, but wanting to hang out with people from church!* We find a spot in the back of a bar around the corner and are delighted to discover that Irish traditional musicians hold a session each Sunday night. Beers are ordered all around, and I sit, shining a bit with sweat from the dish doing and brimming with warm joy. These people like each other. They want to drink beer and talk about theology or joke about things entirely untheological. They want to be friends.

In the coming weeks, we settle into habits. A small core of folks always stays behind to finish up the details of cleanup—recording attendance in the welcome book Rachel made, counting the modest offering of crumpled bills. Napkins and tablecloths go into a bag that Rachel drops off at a twenty-four-hour laundry place on the way to the bar. But at some point the laundromat closes; I begin strapping the bag of laundry to the back of my bike after church and wheeling it along to the bar, so I can toss it in the washing machine after pedaling to my building on the Upper West Side at the end of the night. After drinks, I turn on my bike lights, make my way across Manhattan on Ninth Street until I burst out onto the Hudson, and follow the river all the way home.

In a year or so we'll strike out, with Pastor Phil's encouragement, into the next stage of our life as a church: a nomadic period in which we'll move across the East River to Brooklyn, to the fellowship hall of a crumbling Episcopal church on the corner of Fourth Ave and Pacific. Four weeks later we'll learn that the building has more deferred maintenance than anyone realized, and will soon be condemned. And so we'll move right back out and worship in a congregants' apartment for a while, then find a space as renters at a friendly Zen center, where we'll all take off our shoes for Dinner Church.

Despite my fears, I'll become a pastor. The bishop will

ordain me with Daniel's, Donald's, Pastor Phil's, and so many others' hands laying heavy on my shoulders and head. The next day, I'm installed as the Pastor of St. Lydia's in the Zen center, by two bishops wearing miters and socked feet as we all sit cross-legged on meditation cushions, holding bowls of soup.

We'll lose our office space three different times, once just before Holy Week, causing me to burst into exhausted tears. We'll jam into congregants' apartments for community meetings and go over our budget and giving goals, handing out pledge cards Rachel has hand-stamped with spoons and forks. Rachel will start the Enough for Everyone Community Garden in a vacant lot, and we'll grow our own vegetables in raised beds set on centuries of rubble and broken glass.

All that is ahead of us. But from that first spring, here is what I remember: riding home along the river with the laundry strapped to my bike, and coming over the crest of the hill to discover the cherry trees have burst into bloom along the Seventy-ninth Street boat basin. In the night they look ghostly under the streetlamps, boats gently bobbing on the waves.

Each week the same homeless man sleeps on a bench beneath the petaled trees. Sometimes I have leftovers from church—curried chickpeas and a hunk of our communion bread in a clean yogurt container—so I stop and set it next to him as an offering. Then I climb back on my bike and ride home, against the tide of the mighty river, as the petals fall and cover him while he sleeps.

II

Enough

And we pray, not
for new earth or heaven, but to be
quiet in heart, and in eye,
clear. What we need is here.

—Wendell Berry

Cardboard Wings

"Come, one and all!"

Charlotte summons us, declaring her invitation to the night wind. It's Christmas Eve, and we're standing at Fourth Avenue and Union Street between an Exxon station and an overflowing sidewalk garbage can. Beside us, traffic barrels along the avenue, taxis bearing down on their horns.

"Come, shepherds and sheep!" Charlotte yells over the din. "Come, kings and sages and magi. Come, all who are wise and all who are foolish. Come!"

Our ragtag band (accordion, guitar, and trombone) pipes up, careening through the melody of "O Come, All Ye Faithful." We toot along as fifteen or so brave congregants lift their voices in exultation and two drunk guys tumble out of a corner dive bar, shouting expletives, lurching at each other aggressively.

Behind us, a semitruck pulls into the gas station, misses the sharp turn, and backs up, engine roaring into reverse. Next to me, a congregant is pulling extra hats and gloves out of her bag, already shivering. The semi lets out a great belch of black smoke from its muffler.

It's possible this was a bad idea.

We dreamed up the St. Lydia's Christmas Eve Pageant Parade because we can't be in our usual space on Christmas. A few weeks ago, I pitched the parade to Rachel and our interns as a festive spectacle, marching across Brooklyn in our makeshift costumes, singing carols.

A few years into our scrappy church project, St. Lydia's has moved across the Brooklyn Bridge and landed at the Zen center. We've grown, stabilized, and even attracted Ezra and Zachary, two seminarians who want to learn from the chaos of church planting. Zachary is a dreamy student at Union Theological Seminary—a multi-instrumentalist from a multiracial family, with tight coils of hair and a five o'clock shadow. Ezra, who often has a slim book of poetry tucked under his arm or in his pocket, has a shaved head, a growing beard, and a heaviness in his countenance.

At his first Dinner Church service, he asked to speak to me during cleanup.

"I just wanted to let you know that things have become a little crazy in my life," he told me, rubbing a hand along a crease in his forehead. "My wife just asked for a divorce. Last week." He started his internship anyway, doing his best to hold things steady for himself and his two small daughters.

Ezra likes the idea of the pageant parade. "Joseph and Mary wandered," he offered when I brought it up. "They were pilgrims when they looked for room at the inn." Maybe he empathized, in the midst of his own destabilizing experience.

"Everyone's gonna be *freezing*" was Rachel's comment. "And *grumpy*." So we decided to end our procession at a warm pub with snacks and beer. Problem solved! Maybe we'd even pick up some neighbors as we went—people stopping for a few minutes to listen to the story or even join in on a carol.

All through Advent, I had preached about the fundamentally disorienting promise of God's incarnation. The story of Christmas is not about Mary and Joseph taking an idyllic journey through the desert on the back of a donkey, I told the congregation, but of life coming apart at the seams. Mary is a young woman from a poor town who has a good thing going: someone wants to marry her. A woman in that time was entirely dependent on either her family or her husband for income and security. Without them, she'd end up out in front of a gate somewhere, begging for spare coins, or mooching off an uncle or cousin for the rest of her life. But Mary was set. She had cut a path toward a secure future. And then God showed up and threw everything off course with a totally worn-out cliché: becoming a teenage mother. Saying yes to God meant risking everything. The meager living she and her husband would earn, their new life together, the possibility for better things. When Mary says yes, she abandons everything for God.

"This is a story of disorientation," I preached as December deepened, "not a cozy tale of a baby in a manger." The Christmas Eve Pageant Parade seemed like an opportunity to travel the streets as Mary and Joseph did, and make our Christmas just a touch less comfortable.

That was the vision. But now, desperately looping carols over the idling of semis as my congregants shuffle their feet to stay warm, I experience a sudden hit of terror. It's possible we've gone too far. The temperature plummeted yesterday and everyone is already freezing. Commuters are rushing out of the subway stop across the street, brushing by our ragtag band without a second glance as they pop their coat collars up against the wind, and scuttle home. No one is curious.

Well, I think, launching into the melody of "God Rest You Merry, Gentlemen," *if a lack of comfort is what we wanted, we've got it.*

Charlotte (who stuck around despite the meager attendance at her first service) rehearses the crowd, teaching us to baa and moo like barnyard animals. She enlists Ezra's elder daughter, Anna, to carry a star on a stick. James, a British sociologist who always looks doleful, is positioned behind Ula's wheelchair, wearing a dish towel on his head, ready to push her along. Ula sports a battered Santa hat.

Jason, an engineer, has constructed a towering angel puppet by hinging together two long cardboard mailing tubes and affixing white satin fabric and silver spray-painted wings. He stands at the edge of the crowd, pulsing the cardboard tubes on their hinges. The angel flaps like a gentle, looming bird.

I hand around glass vigil candles, the kind you place on outdoor shrines. Each congregant is supposed to carry one in our procession, creating a beautiful scene as we follow our path through Brooklyn. But as soon as I have mine lit, it's whipped out by the wind. Everyone else is having the same problem, standing in huddles, hands cupped around the flames. Finally we give up. My congregants look at me, defeated.

Okay, I think. *It is what it is. Let's start.*

Charlotte beckons us along Union, and off we go. We stagger along, plunging into the relative darkness of a more industrial corner of Brooklyn. By day the area exhibits medium-level grit and grime—nothing out of the ordinary for New York City. By night, however, it looks like the set of a true crime show. James pushes Ula's wheelchair stalwartly over shattered glass and crushed beer cans.

"Glo-o-o-o-o-ooooo-o-o-o-o-ooooo-o-o-o-o-ooooo-RIA," we sing, fighting to join our voices as the wind picks up and whips them away. Ezra's younger daughter, Isla, three years old and wearing angel wings over her winter coat, buries her head in her father's neck as he carries her.

"Daddy," I hear her say, "I'm so cold!"

This is the moment when I know I've made a terrible mistake. *Oh God,* I think. *I've ruined Christmas.*

We grind to a halt on the corner of Bond and Butler, across from the brick public housing units called the Gowanus Houses. They're kitty-corner from my new apartment, where I've moved to be closer to St. Lydia's. I walk these blocks all the time, and find them friendly and connected. Neighbors stop to chat with one another on the sidewalk. Men hold forth in front of the bodegas, calling out to friends passing by or giving a dog a scratch behind the ears.

Tonight, though, the bodegas are closed up. The stoops are empty, and I notice only a few scattered windows lit in the apartment buildings. It seems almost everyone has gone away for Christmas, headed to see family someplace else. The feeling left behind, like a residue, isn't so cheerful. The neighborhood is in a different mood tonight, thick and desolate. We're standing there on the corner in tinsel halos and spray-painted wings. Suddenly I feel incredibly naïve. I chose a route that would take us by the Gowanus Houses because we are all one neighborhood, and all part of God's story. But standing on the emptied sidewalk, I feel like a stranger. Our story feels flimsy next to the reality of this block. It seems terribly presumptuous for us to tell it here, when we walk these blocks but don't live on them.

On that street corner, Charlotte tells the story of the angel who visits Mary to inform her that she'll bear the child of God.

"Most favored one, the angel called her," Charlotte

says, "and Mary wondered how it was that she, young, poor, and knocked up, was favored."

Charlotte tells us about Mary's song of revolution—of the new creation being knit together in her womb. *The powerful have been brought down from their thrones,* she sings, *and the rich are sent away empty.* She tears down the empire with her words.

I wonder what our jovial, well-fed church has to say about the hungry being filled or the powerful being torn from their thrones. What can we claim to understand about this story? What can *we* say that the teenage girl on the sixth floor of the houses hasn't already lived?

Mary's song is my favorite passage in the Bible. I return to her words; they remind me what it means to be Christian. But standing here, I'm not sure if this story belongs to me.

Most highly favored lady, we sing, and turn our faces north. I wonder if I'm the only one who's shaken.

The next stop is outside the Brooklyn Inn, a bar on Hoyt Street. I thought carefully about the route, even walked it a few times to make sure it was the right distance. It's just a few blocks, really, from the corner of Union over to Bergen and Smith Street. Fifteen minutes, maybe? What I didn't calculate, however, was the pace of a small herd of grown-ups, multiple children, and a person in a wheelchair shuffling down the sidewalk, stopping at every crossing to wait for the walk signal, while singing. It feels like we've been out here for hours.

At least this part will be cheerful, I think as we approach the friendly striped awning of the bar. Multicolored Christmas lights glow inside. I often stop here for a drink with friends, and it's always a mellow crowd. We process up to the corner and hold position outside, lustily singing "We Three Kings."

On the second verse, a band of drunken, bearded men assemble in the doorway and begin to leer at us. "Merrrrry Christmas," they crow, beer sloshing out of their pint glasses.

"MERRY CHRISTMAS!" we all say, suddenly aware that we're wearing dish towels.

"We're telling the Christmas story," Charlotte tells them, and launches into the bit about the star rising in the east.

"I don't give a FUCK about fucking CHRISTMAS!" one of them exclaims belligerently, pointing a finger at us, punctuating his statement with a swig of his beer.

"And they knelt down and paid him homage!" Charlotte shouts to us through a forced grin, "and then they went down the street to the next stop. *Merry Christmas!*" She shuffles us down the block, men crowing behind us.

This is a nightmare, I think, cheeks burning behind my scarf.

At our final station, the corner of Smith Street, the script instructs us to place our candles together in a makeshift shrine, as if in front of the manger.

I envisioned this as a quiet moment at the end of our sojourn. We would sing "In the Bleak Midwinter," one of my all-time favorite Christmas carols. "What can I give him?" the hymn asks. "Give him my heart," comes the answer. I've written a prayer for Charlotte to read as the hymn concludes. "We bring you our hearts. Our whole life, which you know better than even we do. We bring you the fullness of who we are." It will be beautiful.

As our parade gathers together and the guitar begins to play, I flit from person to person, relighting our candles for this climactic moment. We place them on the pavement. They all immediately go out. Huddled together, more for warmth than for anything else, we begin the hymn. "In the bleak midwinter," we sing, "frosty wind made moan.... Snow had fallen, snow on snow, snow on snow."

"We bring you our hearts," Charlotte begins, teeth audibly chattering. I'm too cold to think about anything but my frozen fingers and toes. Passengers emerge from the Bergen Street subway station and lift their hoods against the wind, ignoring us with the practiced skill of longtime New Yorkers. No one stops to sing a carol.

Warming up in the bar afterward, I laugh and chat with congregants while an oily feeling of humiliation settles in my gut. "Merry Christmas," I chortle, hugging someone who's off to a party at a friend's house. Anna is dancing around, tapping everyone on the head with her star on a stick. Isla chases after her. I watch them, smiling, but part of me wants to crawl under the table.

By now I've befriended the discomfort of my role as a pastor. It's gotten no easier, as a thirty-something Brooklynite, to confess that you believe in God and invite people to sit around a table, take hands, and pray. *This is really dumb,* a voice whispers in your mind. *Nobody believes in God anymore.* It's like sidling along a diving board at thirteen while everyone watches your half-naked, prepubescent body and waits for you to jump.

Tonight, though, I feel something different. I hoped for an experience of beauty and tenderness, our candles lit as we moved through the borough. I hoped for a sense of connection with our neighborhood, of serendipity and surprise. Instead we experienced only wind, darkness, and drunk people. I was a director whose show had too many flaws. When the stage lights were angled wrong, you could see the wires and the rigging—that the sets were just cardboard and the costumes were flimsy. There wasn't any magic here.

My congregants had trusted me enough to follow me, and I brought them through barbed wire and broken glass. I had probably given two small children frostbite. Ula, most likely, will get pneumonia. On Christmas Eve.

"It's fine," I tell myself. "We're all here, and celebrating." But I fret internally, as a congregant tells me a story I've lost the thread of, that it doesn't feel anything like Christmas.

An emperor makes up his mind that the world should be registered. While he sits at a banquet table feasting on pheasant and calling for more wine, a couple of just-married kids are wandering the streets of a strange city when the girl's water breaks. They end up in a stranger's stable, blood and water mingling with the hay as Mary bears down in pain. There's no mama or auntie to squeeze her hand or tell her when to push.

Historians say that there actually was no census when Jesus was born. Some guy named Quirinius held one ten years after Herod died, but Luke insists Jesus was born during Herod's reign. Luke wants to show that Jesus' birth takes place in the middle of displacement and desperation.

The Gospels tell other stories about Mary. In Matthew's version, she and Joseph flee to Egypt because Herod has promised to kill this newborn child. The holy family become refugees, traveling miles over land with the baby strapped to Mary's back. She raises her child in a foreign nation, surrounded by a garble of languages she can't understand. They have no friends, no family—no one to welcome them.

Christmas is about how God is born in forgotten places. It's about families forced to undertake a journey they can't afford at the worst possible time. The powerful men of this world puff and tut about decisions they deem necessary or reasonable, moving pieces on maps or signing their decrees. Meanwhile, in the far-flung corners of their kingdoms, mothers tuck their children in arms and clamber into boats or trucks that will take them across the sea or barbed-wire borders. They pay the bribes, strap their babies into orange life vests. They have been told there is a better life on the other side where their kids can grow up free.

Mary was a brown-skinned Middle Eastern teenager who gave birth alone among animals. She was a poor, despised religious and ethnic minority living in a backwater town under the rule of a powerful and unjust empire. In the years since then, the White Men of History have wrapped her in a clean blue cloth and painted her skin lily-white—a blue-eyed virgin looking up toward heaven. But Mary was all strength and sinew, bite and courage. She was more like the girls that live on the corner of Bond and Butler. Young and dark-skinned. Living in public housing. Unmarried and knocked up. Unimportant to the White Men of History. They'd look at Mary and call her a welfare queen. Put her on line to wait for food stamps. Give her a subpar education. Brand her illegal and send her back to the border.

We don't call women like her holy.

As her first lullaby, Mary sings a song that unseats tyrants. *God will tear down the mighty from their thrones.* Remembering this, we might not be surprised to learn that her Hebrew name, Mariam, means not only "bitterness" but also "rebellion."

As a child, I wore my fair share of cardboard wings and tinsel halos. In third grade, I was an angel in the pageant, wearing a white choir robe. As an infant I even played Jesus, placed in a hay-lined trough as the sixteen-year-old who had been cast as Mary leaned away from me, worried she might make me cry.

We play out the scene every year in our churches: as

soothing and predictable as a bedtime story. God is in heaven, Jesus born on earth, a star hangs above, all is well with the world. For a moment on those Christmas Eves, it seems that all must be well. God is here, as innocent as a child. For some churches, whose congregants inhabit lives of comfort and ease, it can be a story to hide behind. All *is* well for them. They have what they need and can get what they want.

For others, who labor under the grinding weight of minimum-wage jobs, who worry their dark-skinned teen-age boy is looking awfully grown up, who wait for the knock of ICE at the door, the story is not only a salve but a call to arms. God is born, the story says, and the woman who bears him calls for your liberation. It's Mary, that dirt-poor teenage mother, who shows us the paradox of God. To find God, we go not up, to the emperors and rulers of this world, but down. To Mary.

A few years from now, I'll walk the streets we walked tonight with a phone in my hand, checking Facebook to see how many likes some post got. It will be dark, late at night, and I'll be almost to my apartment when I pause to type out a comment, leaned up against a neighbor's wrought-iron fence. In that moment, I will feel a cold, round object pressed to the left side of my head and a hand wrap around my right hand—the one holding my phone.

For a moment, he and I stand as if we are a couple on

a dance floor, his body just behind mine, my hand in his, extended. *Gimme your phone gimme me your phone,* he says clearly, right in my ear, as he slips it from my hand and then *gimme your bag gimme your bag,* and he takes ahold of the shoulder strap and lifts my heavy satchel from me, spinning me out from beneath it with a guiding hand on the small of my back. In one deft move, he gives me a firm but gentle push to send me walking down the sidewalk, away from him.

I am shaking in fear. I turn back for just a moment to see that he's not even running. He's ambling away from me. He's taken my phone and the bag that contains my wallet, my computer, the keys to my apartment, and my passport.

I tremble for days. A week later, after putting on heels and boarding the subway, I collapse into tears. I feel trapped in the shoes, unable to move quickly enough to escape attack. To this day, I startle unpleasantly when a runner comes up behind me on the sidewalk.

Despite these signs of trauma, I feel no ill will toward the man who mugged me. The moment seemed oddly neutral—devoid of any sense of violent intent. Days later, someone finds my keys on the ground, a half block from the encounter, and, noticing my key chain for my local gym, drops them off there, where they have my number on file. My mugger had tossed them on the sidewalk. It felt like he left them so I might find them. I never saw his face, but we shared this intimate moment. His hand on the small of my back, as if we were dancing. I was terrified, but I never felt like I was in danger.

The White Men of History don't give a kid like him a lot of chances. A school system designed to ferry him to prison, a neighborhood designed to deliver him to drug dealers.

We don't call men like him holy.

In the pub, I sit with my beer, watching congregants wish each other a merry Christmas. One by one, they say good-bye and plunge out the door and into the night. Charlotte's working the brunch shift at Balthazar tomorrow before heading back to see her family in Vermont. Ezra will deliver the girls to their mom and then return to his apartment—his first Christmas on his own. James keeps watch at the window for Ula's Access-A-Ride, which will carry her back to the nursing home. Down the street at my darkened studio apartment, a smattering of Christmas cards are stuck to the fridge. From them smile babies and toddlers in matching shirts and onesies, grasping stockings or candy canes.

Here we all are, people with lives that are patchy and at times unmanageable. We hold things together with bits of string and spare parts, and keep moving day to day, because that's what you do. Tonight, we pushed our way over broken glass to tell a story about God coming to dwell in circumstances that were uncertain and untenable, when everything was falling apart at the seams. There was a place at the inn, but the wind still battered at the door.

When you ask for an uncomfortable Christmas, you don't get to choose just how uncomfortable it will be. Ours had moved from industrial wasteland through emptied public housing units to a bar devoted to a despairing kind of drunkenness. We traveled through places that had been left behind, and told our story among people who had nowhere else to be. We were as anonymous as Joseph and Mary were on the streets of Bethlehem, everything boarded up for the night. When we stood on those street corners, our wings had seemed, for the first time, wilted and flimsy. Maybe we were a bunch of naïve believers, proclaiming a gospel of the oppressed without the lived experience to back it up.

I had hoped for a night that was magical. God didn't give us magic. But God gave us truth.

"Come all who are wise and all who are foolish," Charlotte had beckoned. I was wise and foolish. Wise enough to be drawn toward the star and foolish enough to fail to understand what it means—that on the other end are both God and Herod, both divinity and genocide. We will be asked to follow that star places we never wished to go.

There are just a few of us left now, and I realize that the long wooden table and benches of the pub are scattered with the remnants of the Pageant Parade: cardboard wings covered in folded coffee filters and barnyard ears hot-glued to drugstore headbands. I collect them all into a big IKEA bag. It's light to carry: nothing but fabric and cotton balls, glitter and glue. There's also the angel, leaned up against the wall, observing the proceedings. Jason is taking the subway an hour home to Astoria. The angel isn't going home with him. I certainly don't feel like walking her back along our route to the Zen center in the cold. I didn't really plan this part so well.

So I decide to take the angel home to my darkened studio. There will be room for her in the corner. We get up and head out into the cold, zipping our coats. Slinging the bag of costumes over my shoulder, I tip the bandleader of the heavenly host forward and through the door, then hoist her onto my shoulder. On the street we hug one another with wishes for a merry Christmas, and wave goodbye as we split off toward our respective subway stops. The angel and I set out toward my empty apartment, her salvaged fabric billowing behind me in the wind.

Three Miracles

Every week there is bread on a table in the middle of the room. But this is not a gathering of St. Lydia's. It's a rehearsal for a radical marching band I've joined. We're called the Rude Mechanical Orchestra. Every Tuesday night, a collection of tattered activists in thrift store sweaters wheel up on bicycles rigged to carry a trombone or saxophone, backpacks stuffed with sheet music. This is where I learn to be an activist. And, to be honest, a Christian.

My first night I hustle down a flight of stairs into a cramped basement studio and open the door to a clatter of noodled notes and overtones. There are four sections: low brass, woodwinds, trumpets, and percussion, all facing toward each other in a sloppy square. In the middle of the room is a wooden table, and on the table there is always a loaf of bread, pulled from someone's bike bag. As more people arrive, other offerings of food are set on this slap-dash altar.

"You eat dumpster-dived?" someone might ask before handing me a blood orange or a slice of black pepper sa-lami, as if they're inquiring if I'm vegetarian or gluten free.

"Yup," I answer, receiving their offering in a cupped hand.

Dumpster diving is illegal, but if you know the right places you can make out like a bandit and feast like a king. Band members bring entire bags of firm grapes, bars of gourmet chocolate, and bags of almonds, all in pristine condition and one day past expiration.

Adjacent to a gaggle of gleaming sousaphones, I sit at the back of the low-brass section with my trombone and survey the room. The players are bearded and scruffy, at ease in their bodies. A clarinetist leans a head on a friend's shoulder and rubs their back. The group is gorgeously Queer, bypassing gender norms. We go around the circle and introduce ourselves with names and our pronouns, a practice that's new to me. I'm supposed to manage to memorize both, which feels daunting. From there, band members take turns leading rehearsals. Changes are scrib-bled down on sheet music that will inevitably be lost in the cavern-like rehearsal space. We spend a good portion of each rehearsal reconstructing what we decided the last time about whether or not we'll repeat the B section.

A lot of the players live in communal houses, sharing kitchens and bathrooms and making big one-pot meals on rotation for everyone. They live cheap so they can dedicate their lives to activism. Practically off the capitalist grid, they buy almost everything used or trade for it, making and repairing household items. They always have someone to crash with. Their support networks extend across the country and around the world.

It strikes me that their lives look more like what Jesus was talking about than just about anything I've ever seen in church. They're like a secular monastery, living like Christians did in the first few centuries, sharing what they earned and making sure everyone was fed.

The Rude Mechanical Orchestra adopts me, despite my lack of body hair. They're always reminding me that we already have everything we need to live. That what looks like deficit to the rest of the world is brimming with abundance to them. Being in the band shows me that what others have thrown away might be enough for a feast.

Jesus, too, had a habit of making enough from a little. Some spit on his hand and a scrape of dirt are enough to make a blind man see. That's all he needs. A few loaves of bread and a couple of fish become a meal for a multitude. When the wine runs low, turns out water can serve in a pinch. The most important thing is that the party keep going. It doesn't matter how little you've got, somehow it's enough when God's at the table.

I didn't join the Rude Mechanical Orchestra to become a better Christian, though. I was hoping to make friends with someone who wasn't part of my church. Or maybe, just *maybe*, meet someone who didn't send me 3:00 A.M. texts that read, "hey wut R U doin U hot baby."

Things are rough on the dating front. There are some for whom the Pastor Thing is a no-go. Others seem to fetishize my role, or imagine I can heal or redeem them. One, who initially seemed attracted to my sense of power and authority, turned out to be threatened by it. Another had a subconscious notion that dating a woman of the cloth would make him a better person and fetter the rage he carried. These relationships started out with fiery intensity before explosively flaring out in showers of fights and fireworks.

Now I'm in a long dry spell, punctuated by first dates that rarely produce a second. I zip myself into alluring clothes, feeling like a carbon copy of myself, and try to arrange my body into pleasing, nonchalant poses. I'm extraordinarily bad at dating. I have a tendency to ask academic questions that make dates resemble college entrance interviews. Or I go too deep too fast, acting like a pastor instead of a person. "That must have left you feeling really abandoned," I'll say, instead of talking about, I don't know, a movie. I don't understand how to flirt. I always text back too soon. I always need too much.

Rachel fields a deluge of fretful anxiety concerning my lack of a dating life. She has men trailing her through the aisle when she's picking up an angled paintbrush, or asking for her number on the R train, and seems to be an expert on all things attraction.

"You're dressing like a church lady," she tells me bluntly one day and drags me off to shop. In an effort to up my

game, she stuffs me into skinny jeans and a leather jacket
and tells me I look cute. I believe her. I can't even tell how
wrong I feel.

They're afraid you'll try to convert them, Mieke says.

They assume you don't have sex, my friend Tim offers.

You just haven't met the right person, another friend
opines. She is, as yet, unjaded.

I get drunk and make out at parties and on street corners. I log on to OkCupid and upload the few pictures of
me not at church. I revise my profile, reaching for a voice
that doesn't sound propped up or needy. In return, pictures
of strangers' dicks show up every morning in my inbox. I
write people and never hear back. I hear back, then tell
them I'm a pastor, and then never hear back. We kiss, but
they never call back. Maybe they thought better of it.

It's funny how deficiency and abundance can live side
by side. My life is rich in so many ways. Everything around
me is beautiful: tables piled with home-cooked meals and
a church full of smart, thoughtful people. There is enough
of so much, and more than enough. But pastors experience
a strange doubleness. Our relationships with congregants
are a one-way street. Our role is a professional one, like a
counselor and a teacher rolled into one. I am often vulnerable with the Lydians, but I can't call them up after a bad
day for a good cry. It would muddy the waters of our relationship, make them feel they have to care for me. I created a church because I was lonely, but in the act of leading
it, I've ended up alone.

A thought won't stop nagging at me, like a persistent

mosquito. *Maybe there's something wrong with you.* The only thing in my life that doesn't feel like enough is me.

The Miracle of 304 Bond Street

The real-estate agent and I stand together inside the empty storefront. Ductwork runs overhead like a network of highway overpasses. The fuse box hangs open. In the back left corner the agent shows me the bathroom: a lone, exposed toilet standing next to a sink hookup.

"Just put up some drywall and you're done!" he tells me optimistically.

The place is big and the light is good, but it costs eight thousand dollars a month.

"We'll need proof of your company's income," he informs me briskly. "The landlord asks for eighty times the monthly rent."

Reluctantly, I multiply eight thousand dollars times eighty in my head.

"Sure!" I tell him, brightly. And then, "But we're not a company. We're a church?"

"Um-hm," he counters, pulling out his BlackBerry.

"So our income won't be meeting those requirements."

"Well, you can always fill out the application and see what they say," he says with a half-hearted shrug. He holds out a stack of papers with a corporate logo printed across the top.

"Great. Thanks."

This is the fourth, maybe fifth storefront I've looked at

in person, and it's clear I'll need to look for a sixth. The strategy, thus far, is this: Ignore the voice in my head screaming "YOU'RE A FRAUD" while real-estate agents rattle off square footage and heating costs. I nod confidently and ask about security deposits, well aware that our bank account balance currently sits at, like, seventeen dollars.

"You guys have the collateral to do this?" one of them asks me.

"We're running a capital campaign," I say, smiling confidently. It's true! Last week, Rachel printed out the mailing labels on our sputtering desktop printer, and the interns spent the afternoon stuffing and stamping. People will definitely send those pledge cards back in. I'm sure of it.

The name of the game right now is "Faking It." But we've got to make it. St. Lydia's is growing. Each week we stuff people in at the corners of tables or send an intern out for more bread. Finding a place to hold a meeting or a Bible study is a constant struggle in a city where real estate is the most valuable commodity. Our theology circle meets at a bar, where congregants shout about liberation theology over the din.

"WHAT IS CONE SAYING ABOUT OUR THEOLOGICAL ANTHROPOLOGY IN LIGHT OF THE WHITE HISTORY OF ECCLESIOLOGY IN AMERICA?" Burke, the facilitator, screams, while everyone else leans in, cupping their hands around their ears.

I'm dreaming about our own space. A place where we don't have to puzzle-piece our materials for the liturgy into plastic bins after Dinner Church, to be stacked on shelves in a closet. Most important, I want a place where people can see us when they wander by. Where we can hold community gatherings and arts events. Where we can invite someone off the street who hasn't eaten in a while and heat something up in the microwave.

Rachel and I explain all this to Ezra and Zachary, the interns. They nod, dazed, when they hear the plan.

"It seems really big," Zachary says.

"Yes, it does," I say.

"Can we afford something like that?" Ezra asks.

"Good question," I answer. Very good question. We'll need a capital campaign. And an architect. And a contractor. I've never done anything like this before.

In the end, I find 304 Bond Street, not through a commercial real-estate agent, but on Craigslist. Trolling through listings in bed late one night, I see it. A long, narrow storefront with windows on either end, a patch of a garden out back, and a huge basement. The entrance is on the street. It's close to multiple subway lines. The storefront sits in a neighborhood that is mixed economically, where anyone who might want to come to our church will feel comfortable. No orphaned toilets. No exposed ductwork. Just a clean, white room for four thousand dollars a month.

I walk the few blocks down Bond Street to see the place on a snowy evening. After fiddling with the lock, the real-estate agent pushes the door open and we step inside the empty, echoing room. The overhead lights haven't been installed, so we poke around in the dark with a flashlight, which feels sort of sketchy. But the place is neatly dry-walled, the huge windows in front will let in lots of light, and the yard in the back (mostly rubble) is waiting for something beautiful to happen.

I ask to see the basement. The agent (who by the way is wearing leopard-print stretch pants and speaks in a thick Russian accent) tells me it's flooded right now and we can't go down there. But the landlord is going to pump it out. "No problem," she tells me.

It's the best space we've seen. There are discussions with congregants and visits from members of our Leadership Table. A week later, I've just landed in Los Angeles for a young clergy conference when the property manager calls. "If you want it, you'd better move fast, because someone else is interested."

This feels like a hoax, but it's New York, it's just how things work. Panic ensues. Calls back and forth. Helpless in California, I send Jake over because the basement is still filled with four inches of water. Jake leads our music program these days, playing the djembe and running rehearsals with the song leaders every week. He is the closest thing to an adult at St. Lydia's. A complete and utter hero, he dons galoshes and ventures down into the basement, ducking under a low beam, then sloshes around taking video.

"Just sent you a video," he texts me. I press play and squint—the footage is mostly darkness and distressing gargly water sounds. "Ummm . . . looks like there's a lot of space down here," Jake narrates. "About up to my ankles in water . . . this seems like a load-bearing beam?" It reminds me of the garbage compactor scene in *Star Wars*. There's got to be a giant snake down there somewhere.

I call the property manager from baggage claim and feign an authoritative voice. *"The basement is still filled with four inches of water and you expect me to sign a lease?"* I yell into the phone, feeling very L.A.

In the end, our hand is forced. The place is cheap, and we don't have better options. They promise the basement will be drained and cleaned by move-in, and they throw in a month's free rent.

A fevered call to Rachel, and she's throwing herself in a cab and driving through a freshly arrived blizzard to sign the lease in the basement of a cigar-smoking landlord. I'm not making this up. Documents are faxed back and forth. Edits are made. We have a place.

Against all odds. Something from nothing. Across the country, I take myself out for a drink to celebrate. My hands are trembling.

The Miracle of the Ice Cream

Our architect tells me that liming the walls will be easy.

"So, how does this work?" I ask her.

"You just go to Lowe's and get some lime, then you mix it up with water and put it in spray bottles. It will turn the brick wall this nice white, which will make the place look bigger. And it's an antibacterial that keeps away bugs."

Keeping away bugs seems like a good investment of

time and money, considering our ample use of food in a city with more rats than people.

"It will be fun," she tells me. "For the community!"

"It will be fun!" I repeat later to Julia, our new staff coordinator, who has been on the job exactly one week.

Julia looks skeptical.

Rachel announced her departure a few months ago, to focus on her artwork and recover in the midst of a health crisis in her family. It was a blow. Her mom had been sick for months and Rachel had been just hanging on. For a while, it felt impossible to imagine St. Lydia's without her. We threw her a big party and I cried a whole lot. She did too.

Then we found Julia, a recent seminary grad obsessed with Harry Styles and, unlike everyone else at St. Lydia's, oddly well informed when it came to pop culture. She loved to cook and was highly extroverted; the awkwardness of the Lydian tables didn't faze her. She was perfect.

By this time, we're still paying rent for both the Brooklyn Zen Center and the new storefront at 304 Bond Street, leaving our bank account chronically endangered. We have a lot on our hands, and liming the walls seems like an unnecessary Martha Stewart moment, if not a potential complete disaster.

But Julia relents. We enlist Clara, a congregant who runs a company making adorable stuffed animals, to spearhead the project. She seems accustomed to crafting on an unwieldy scale. She makes a trip to the hardware store and assembles dust masks, spray bottles, buckets, and a couple thirty-pound bags of lime. I announce at church that one

Thursday evening in June, we'll be liming the walls of the new space, and everyone should come.

When the night in question arrives, I roll up at the storefront on my bike and find Clara crouched in a corner of the empty space, hair pulled back in a bandanna, mixing lime with water and shaking spray bottles.

"It's working pretty well," she reports, showing me a section of the brick wall where she's started spraying. It looks exactly the same as before.

"It seems like it's still red," I observe.

"Yeah . . ." she answers, furrowing her brow. "I think it takes a little time for the lime to take effect."

A little time is no problem. I pull a portable speaker from my tote bag and get some music going. Congregants begin to filter in, poking their heads through the glass door and marveling at the deliciously open space.

Wendy and Phil arrive—together, I notice. Wendy leads the children's programs at a big church in Manhattan. She's a single mom to Peter, a precocious redheaded child who's not yet in middle school. Phil's a guy with neatly trimmed steely gray hair, and a more colorful background than you might expect. Kicked out of the house at age fifteen, he ended up in the New York City punk scene, and on crew for the Cramps. Now he serves on the church Leadership Table.

Phil opens the door for Wendy. I raise my eyebrows.

"I brought homemade cookies," Wendy says, holding up a wicker basket filled with baked goods, and we all cheer.

Soon the Access-A-Ride rolls up, and we all spill out

of the door to help as Ula is lowered on the van's hydraulic lift. The portable ramps haven't arrived yet, but Ula manages to stand with a congregant on either side of her while someone else lifts her wheelchair the two steps into the storefront. She steps in painstakingly behind it.

Things have worsened for Ula on a few fronts. She had a stroke and somehow landed in a hospital in Connecticut. When she returned to New York, it became clear that her personality had shifted. She was softer and more gregarious, less interested in stirring up trouble. Her barbed comments had been worn down to nubs. She had difficulty moving the right side of her body, and her speech was stilted and slow. James and Charlotte took a shine to her. "She loves drugstore novels and nail polish," Charlotte told us during announcements at church, encouraging us to visit and send her cards.

Ula still had a litany of complaints, especially about her care wherever she was staying. And who wouldn't—she was living in nursing homes where the average patient spoke not one word. Together the Lydians and I visited her social workers, amplifying her requests for physical therapy or visits to specialists. She was always in a state of emergency—all her belongings were left at the last hospital, or her phone had gone missing again, or her disability checks had stopped coming. Solve one problem, and another popped up. Our resources always felt paltry in the face of her need.

One weekday afternoon I joined her at Mount Sinai Hospital for a meeting with her neurologist. The three of us sat in his office, peering at pictures of Ula's brain, illuminated by a light box.

"When will . . . I be . . . back . . . the way I was?" she struggled to say.

"Ula," he told her. "You've been through multiple aneurysms and surgeries. Now a stroke. The fact that you even *have* speech . . . well, it's something of a miracle."

Ula and I share the same birthday, October 24, only she's exactly twenty-five years older than I am. We also attended the same college. I sometimes made a point of sharing this fact with newcomers to the church when we met for coffee. They always startled. It startled me too.

Maybe Ula looks at me and sees a reflection of the person she should've been. I look at her and see a reflection too: of the person I could be. By some twist of fate, she's the one in a nursing home.

Tonight, arranged back in her chair safely inside 304 Bond Street, Ula regards us all one by one.

"Hi, hi," she says, waving with queenly dignity and nodding her head. "I'm sorry."

"Ula, you don't have to be sorry!" we chorus.

Clara arms her with a squeeze bottle. She scoots over to a section of wall and begins spraying with her good hand.

The thing is, when you're liming a wall and the wall doesn't change colors, it's hard to tell where you've limed and where you haven't. Our architect had instructed me that we should try to achieve "three even coatings," a request that seemed reasonable at the time. Now, though, with nine volunteers spraying the walls haphazardly, it's clear we'll end up with a wall that looks like it has the measles.

They're having fun, though. Julia and Wendy perch at the tops of the ladders left by the contractors, spraying along the ceiling line, while another congregant, Dan, takes a more random approach, spritzing indiscriminately as he tells a story. Everyone is bopping around to the music. It's a warm summer night and we don't have the benefit of air-conditioning; we work up a sweat.

When the light begins to fade, we decide that we've done something equivalent to three coats and float outside to the stoop, sipping bottles of water and chatting. I'm leaning back on a hand pressed into the grit of the sidewalk, about to throw my head back in laughter at a joke Julia just cracked, when an ice cream truck pulls up, sounding its well-worn tune.

"Hey, guys," says the ice cream man, cutting the music and leaning out the window. "You all want some free ice cream? It's my last day on the job!"

Apparently, he's going out with a bang. He plunges his hands into the freezers, pulling out Firecrackers and King Cones and ice cream sandwiches and tossing them toward our waiting, sweaty hands. There is ice cream for everyone. More than we can eat. More than enough, more than we deserve; a grace so easy and wholesome and pure, it falls on us like manna.

Something from nothing.

The Miracle of the Baptism

Zachary's mom forgot to baptize him. By the time he discovers it, he's been an intern at St. Lydia's for half a year, and a seminarian for two. Zachary's dreamy calm is interrupted by little. But he's not happy.

"They did my brother," he tells me at a supervisory meeting, "but then 'things got busy.' That's actually what my mom said!"

"Geez," I tell him, grimacing. "I'm so sorry."

Zachary looks up through his lashes. "Do you think you could baptize me?"

I grin.

"Of *course* we can baptize you!"

We pick a date in July, which turns out to be our second Sunday at 304 Bond Street. Zachary is thrilled, smiling and eagerly planning meetings with his baptismal sponsors. The problem is, our space isn't ready. And when I say it isn't ready, I don't mean that the light fixtures haven't arrived or something like that. I mean that the wood flooring has not yet been laid. I mean that there is no kitchen to speak of. I mean that there is no source of running water other than the spigot in the basement.

Julia and I draw up a set of crazed arrangements to feed fifty people with no floor and no kitchen, and baptize Zachary in a church with no font and, in fact, no water. We do have a working bathroom with a door. So there's that. And the limed walls turned out really pretty.

After cooking up an army's worth of pasta and salad at home, Wendy spoons it all into aluminum trays and loads them into a granny cart, to be transported by Phil to church. This particular granny cart, borrowed from Julia, is rickety, with a tendency to throw a wheel at an unexpected moment. So it is that a portion of Zachary's baptism dinner is offered to the streets of Brooklyn, always hungry for the detritus of lost objects or, in this case, entire feasts.

Phil flies in the door, breathless and panicked, telling us what happened. We unload the remaining trays of food and send someone down the block for more bread, just as Zachary's family arrives, en masse from New Mexico, alongside a group of ten corn-fed visitors from a church in Iowa. They are welcomed at the door by Hannah, wearing a long flowery skirt, feet bare and hair hanging down her back. She helps them fill out name tags.

We all wear name tags at St. Lydia's. It's something I'm glad for because, until recently, Hannah went by a different name, and I'm still worried I'll let the old one slip out by accident. After worship one evening she took me aside (though she went by another pronoun at that time) and told me in a soft voice that she was trans, and starting to transition. Over the next few months, her baggy jeans and comic book T-shirts were replaced by skirts and colorful tops, and her shell of shyness fell away, revealing a quirky, clever woman. She started speaking up more in church, and writing hilarious reflections on Facebook. She was blossoming. Now she stands at the door, handing out name tags and markers, her own name pinned to her chest.

"Thank you so much, Hannah!" one of the Iowans says,

and I see the corners of Hannah's mouth lift just slightly, into an imperceptible but delighted smile.

Everyone mills around in our thousand square feet of unfinished storefront, unsure where to put their backpacks or how to help. Julia and a few congregants spread the tablecloths on the floor, as if we're holding a picnic, and set up an impromptu buffet on a piece of plywood balanced across two sawhorses. Ezra asks someone to keep an eye on the girls, and he and I trudge down to the basement, heave open the sidewalk hatch, and push through the giant, galvanized metal washtub St. Lydia's employs as a font, which I stick in the middle of the sidewalk. The basement, by the way, is now clean and dry. The contractors laid down new concrete and dug a sloppy trench around the perimeter that slopes down to a sump pump that's constantly gurgling, siphoning away the water that seeps in through the walls. Sometimes it loses its will to continue and gives up, dark water pooling around it. My relationship to the sump pump seems overly involved, like it's another member of staff—a problem employee who's always giving me trouble.

Ezra passes me the hose, and I yell down to him to turn on the water. It sputters and spurts, then runs into the tub in a clear, cold stream.

Charlotte, song leader for the night, begins to sing. "Come, every seeking soul!" and I clamber into place, adjusting my stole.

Our messy crew circles the washtub and begins lighting our candles, passing the flame from one person to the next. Zachary stands next to the tub, barefoot, dressed in loose white clothing. The song ends and our voices die away, leaving a residue of charged electricity. We stand with anticipation, on the edge of this microcosmic body of water, waiting to see someone reborn.

By our baptism into the death and resurrection of your Son Jesus Christ, I chant, *you turn us from the old life of death-dealing ways and make us new.*

I take Zachary's hand and he steps into the frigid water.

"What do you seek?"

"Life in Christ."

"Do you renounce the evil powers of this world that rebel against God?"

"I renounce them."

There are more questions. More defiant statements that Zachary and we who witness his baptism are no friends to evil.

I scoop a pitcher full of water from the font and pour it over Zachary's head, one, two, three times. He shudders compulsively; the water is as a cold as the ocean. Then we wrap him in a towel, and come inside singing to eat dinner cross-legged on the floor.

This is the miracle: that there is never enough, yet always enough. With no kitchen, no floors, and no table, we can feed fifty people and baptize someone along the way. We have nothing but an empty room, a lit candle, a bucket of water, and a loaf of bread, but it's enough to claim Zachary as a child of God.

Around this time I go on a date. We sit opposite each other, sipping our matching cups of frothy drinks. I really like him. He asks college interview questions just like I do. We talk about performance art and ritual. Then I tell him I'm a pastor, and a door slides closed behind his eyes. The date hadn't been over, but it is now. We lurch through the rest of the conversation until he can make a half-excusable exit. My cheeks are hot and red.

I know I am too easily crushed. I go home and keep looking at his picture even though I shouldn't. I hope he'll write, even though I shouldn't.

I try telling them before the date. I try telling them after the date. It is never a selling point.

Every unanswered text, every guy who said he'd call and didn't, is added to a growing folder of evidence in my mind labeled "You're Completely Undatable." My clerical garb becomes a symbol for all of it: the formless black uniform, the white collar. Its message: "Do Not Cross." Freud spoke of the Madonna-whore complex; I'm living it out. Men, it seems, want their God and sex separate.

I remind myself that my worth isn't based on men who aren't interested in me. But when you keep getting low scores from strangers, it's hard not to think of yourself as a low score. Online, I get a message a week from middle-aged couples in Yonkers or White Plains who wonder if I will join them to "explore a new side of their relationship." (The answer is no.) I get messages from boomers in Greenwich who are clearly married and looking for something on the side.

I blow-dry my hair. I put on eye makeup. I try to care about outfits. I try not to need so much. I wonder why one half of my life is so full and the other half so empty. It starts to feel like maybe God designed it that way. In which case I'm pretty mad at God.

Last week the windows leaked during a rainstorm and soaked all the kids' artwork on display. As I was sopping up the rainwater with towels, Harrison, a local homeless guy who stops by every four days or so with a long story, always at an inopportune time, burst through the door, smelling of alcohol.

"Harrison, I've got a lot on my hands right now," I told him from the floor, where I crouched on my hands and knees between a pile of towels.

"Oh, I know, I know," he said, "I know you're too busy for the likes of me." He stood at the door, poised like he was ready to leave, laying it on thick. "I never wanted to be an inconvenience, I really didn't."

"Harrison, you're not an inconvenience," I snapped at him. "Just come and sit down on the benches and I can help you when I'm done."

Too busy. It's a phrase I've started hearing from more congregants than Harrison, and it breaks my heart every time I hear it. "I know you're really busy, but do you think we could have coffee sometime?"

Every day I am faced with lack: the needs of our space

and my people, the finite quality of time, the disappointing reality of myself. My bad mood can break a new congregant's heart.

"I got myself into this," I reason. "I'm the one who decided to try something so ambitious."

I lock the doors after an evening meeting and am home by 9:30, eating cold takeout. There was always enough, but now I'm not so sure.

We usually think of abundance as having a lot: an overflowing cornucopia on Thanksgiving, a sumptuous wedding feast, maybe cash raining down from a Vegas slot machine. St. Lydia's showed me abundance is a secret hidden inside of scarcity. It lives, tucked inside not-enoughness, waiting to show you that God does not do math. Abundance is discovering God's provision right in the middle of your fret and worry. Even when the bank balance has plummeted and the cupboard seems empty, there's always enough to feed everyone. There are some dry beans and a few carrots in the back of the fridge and we always have bread in the freezer. We can feast on that.

When we first moved into 304 Bond Street, people arrived with bent spoons and wonky forks pillaged from their kitchen drawers. If we could believe that what we need is here in church, maybe we could believe it in all the parts of our lives. Maybe Charlotte could write a one-woman show. Maybe Ezra could make it through his divorce. Maybe we could know our neighbors.

And if we could believe that what we need is here in church, perhaps we could believe it in our lives, or in our nation. God gives us enough for everyone, as long as no one hoards.

One evening after closing up at the storefront I head home, clean up, and put on a fresh set of clothes. I'm meeting someone at a bar—a guy I met through a community meeting a few weeks ago. He seems interested in faith but hasn't come to church (which would render him absolutely off-limits) and isn't relating to me like a pastor. One day, he messages me and asks if I want to meet up sometime.

At the bar, we settle in with a couple of beers. The conversation is running along at top speed, we're both laughing, and I'm leaning in a little closer when a woman opens the door and walks over—long-limbed, easy gait, cascade of glossy hair, glimpse of milky cleavage.

"Hey!" he says to her, wrapping his arm around her slim waist. "Emily, this is my girlfriend."

"Oh!" I say, a slick of embarrassment flooding my system. "It's so nice to meet you."

"You too," she says, perching on the edge of an open chair and drawing close to him. "He keeps telling me about this amazing pastor."

Lost Things

On my thirty-fourth birthday, my mother gives me a gift: a ring that belonged to my great-grandmother. Mom stows it in her purse on the flight from Seattle. Sitting on the couch in my apartment, she presents it to me in a small cardboard jewelry box. Inside, nestled in cotton, is a slim gold band set with a delicate sapphire flanked by two tiny pearls. It's tiny, fitting only on my pinkie finger. Also included is a photograph of my long-dead ancestor in an oval frame. Gazing out from sepia in a high-collared Victorian gown, she bears an unmistakable resemblance to both my mother and me. Something about the angle of her jaw and the look in her eyes.

I love this ring. The thought that it has traveled through three generations of hands and ended up in mine seems almost supernatural. I put it on my finger, imagining that I'm connecting back through space and time to this woman I have never seen or met.

"Is it tight enough on your finger?" my mom asks.

"Yes," I tell her. "It's perfect."

The next morning, the ring shining on my hand, I'm sitting in the windowsill at 304 Bond Street churning through emails when a young woman with bright lipstick rides up on her bike and peers in the window, her helmet tapping on the glass. I get up, set my laptop down, and hang my head out the door.

"Hey!" I say. "How's it going?"

"Oh, hey!" she answers, chagrined that she's been caught peering. She unclips her helmet and pulls it off, a mess of short, dark curls tumbling out. "Can I ask you a weird question?"

The woman, whose name is Melina, spills out a harrowing story that would evoke immediate sympathy from anyone who's ever been a performer. She's the house manager of a performance piece called *The Dreary Coast*, taking place on the canal; just last night, they were booted out of their staging space. They're desperate for another location where they can store costumes and hold warm-ups before the outdoor show. Melina has hit the end of her resources. In desperation, she is riding around the neighborhood looking for a place that might host them, Mary and Joseph style. My inner innkeeper is activated.

"Well, when do you need it?" I ask her.

"Tonight?" she says, cringing.

She's up shit creek, it seems, literally and figuratively.

I've heard about *The Dreary Coast.* It's notable for three reasons. One, the show retells the story of the Greek mythological figure Charon, the ferryman who carries souls across the river Styx to the underworld. The audience sits on a boat that sails down the Gowanus as the actors play their scenes on the waterway's industrial banks. Two, the boat was designed by a street artist named Swoon, whose recent show at the Brooklyn Museum entranced me. And three, the writer and director of this piece is a guy named Jeff, with whom I went on an Internet date years ago. Jeff, like so many others, politely withdrew from our date when he unearthed my religious tendencies, stirring a by-now-familiar cocktail of emotions that included dull hopelessness, disappointed rejection, and unshakable certainty that I would die alone in the traditional manner—my entrails consumed by my cat, clergy collar banded round my neck.

Melina stands no chance of being eaten by anyone's cat, least of all her own. She is beautiful and breathless, her enthusiasm for her work contagious, and her desperation unexpectedly appealing. I want to help. And really, it's hilarious to imagine a play about hell, written by an avowed atheist who once rejected me, being housed in my church. I tell Melina that we need the main space for worship, but if she thinks the basement will work for them, they can move in tonight.

Within hours, a crew rolls up in a truck piled with costumes. The metal doors of the sidewalk hatch are propped open, and the stage crew marches down to the basement, loading in intricate masks and headdresses perched atop Styrofoam heads. Hades's cape is made of some kind of coarse animal fur, and the mask of Cerberus, ferocious with three snarling dog heads, is placed in the shadows. Twenty actors cram themselves inside our moist, mushroomed basement that night, the sump pump spasmodically slurping up the toxic waters of the canal. Upstairs in our main space, Lydian worshippers assemble. We sing "Jesus, We Are Gathered" in four-part harmony while the demons of the underworld lurk below.

Early on in our church experiment, I noticed that a more than usual number of our congregants had lost a parent too young. In their teens or twenties, the one thing that should never disappear, did. Our congregants have no tolerance for bullshit—they won't accept lacquered platitudes in church. So perhaps it is right that, in this season, a shadowed presence lurks beneath our floorboards. They already know it's there.

One thing our basement lacks (in addition to fresh air and natural daylight) is a bathroom, and so, before Charon, Persephone, Hades, and their attending demons head out to the plutonian banks of the Gowanus for the performance, they emerge one by one from downstairs and silently wait to use the toilet. They do so smack in the middle of communion. The actors do their best to be discreet, but, in full costume and makeup, it proves difficult. That first night, as I sing our Eucharistic Prayer, basket of bread in my hands, I look up to see a demon, face painted in terrifying shades of red and black and wearing a set of giant ram horns atop his head, waiting outside the bathroom door. He looks on with curiosity, hands clasped politely in front of him.

"He took a loaf of bread," I sing, "and after blessing it, he broke it, gave it to them, and said, 'Take, this is my body.'" My eyes meet those of the nameless demon, and I find myself, as I so often do while singing our prayers, with a catch in my throat. His countenance is fearsome, but his eyes hold a tender curiosity. I often glimpse this look in people's eyes as I preside, singing a two-thousand-year-old story of a God who finds us in something as ordinary as bread.

Who knows what the demon thought of our bread or our singing? Maybe he saw the same beauty I so often do. Maybe he was perplexed by our devotion to a story he'd never much cared for. Or maybe he just really needed to pee.

The days tick toward Halloween, and the Lydians develop a friendly rapport with the cast. On cold nights they return just as we're closing up from Dinner Church. We ladle leftover soup into bowls and heat it up for them, or find a few beers in the back of the fridge and crack them open. They've caught sight of our world, and I have the chance to catch sight of theirs when, as a thank-you for hosting the show, Melina sets aside a ticket for me. I clamber aboard Charon's boat and sail, with twenty or so other lost souls, down the waters of the canal. An underworldly oarsman navigates our neighborhood river, which seems, from this new perspective on the water, an entirely alien place.

The Greeks imagined the underworld encompassed by five rivers. From the banks of the river Styx, Charon ferried souls from the realm of the living to the realm of the dead. Every soul who travels to the underworld should drink from the river Lethe—the river of forgetfulness and oblivion. When you drink, you forget your life in the world above. Floating on the Gowanus, we're each presented with a tiny silver tumbler. Hoping that they're not really filled with river water, we hold up our glasses and toast each other, drinking away our memories of the world above. Charon begins to row, and we sink deeper into the shadows of the canal. The abandoned cement factory looms before us, fugitive goat lurking within.

We pause along the way, and Persephone boards. Her face looks hollow; she's being ferried straight to Hades, her abductor. He duped her into eating a single pomegranate seed, and now she's bound to stay with him here half the year. The world above goes cold and frozen when she's gone.[1]

I lost my great-grandmother's ring.

It happened the very first day I wore it. Somewhere between brunch with my parents, moving around pumpkins for St. Lydia's Fall Fair, and finding extra toilet paper for the *Dreary Coast* cast in the basement, it slipped off my pinkie finger. No amount of searching with flashlights on hands and knees, posting flyers, or calling the police precinct could bring it back.

"This ring has been passed down through *three* generations," I told a bewildered cast member late that night as I rummaged through a plastic bin in the basement with my cellphone flashlight, "and I lost it after *forty-eight hours.*" All night, I feel physically sick. I dream about it for days afterward, seeing it fall through the rungs of a gutter toward the oblivion of the canal. Some things we lose are gone forever.

It's a lesson we learn young. I remember visiting a Barnes & Noble with my dear friend Nancy's daughter, Maggie, to see if the staff had found her Love You, a tiny stuffed rabbit she carried everywhere with her, until she'd lost it the weekend before. We explained to three-year-old Maggie before the visit that Love You might not be at the store, but when the manager told us that the lost-and-found box did not contain a stuffed rabbit, her despair was violent and unmitigated.

"Why won't you *give it to me?*" she wailed as I carried her from the store.

"Maggie, I don't have it," I told her desperately. "We don't know where it is." Later, buckled into her car seat, her cry pivoted from personal accusation to existential anguish.

"Why won't THEY give it to me?"

And later, rage spent and staring dully out the car window, tears still spattered on her cheeks, she asked simply, "Who will take care of Love You?"

A worn stuffed bunny. A delicate gold ring. Retail value may vary, but these objects are rich with symbolic meaning, and symbols are real. The stuffed bunny rabbit means you're safe. A great-grandmother's ring means you're part of a family. We cling to these objects because they're a kind of shorthand notation that tells us who we are. Without them, we're not so sure.

It was a loss of memory my mom described when she spoke of the death of her own mother. Who would she turn to when she needed to remember the stories? She couldn't recall the twists and turns of her parents' courtship or that funny thing Chrissy said that day of the picnic at Boardman Park. Without Grandma, the stories were gone.

Was Maggie less safe without her Love You? Absolutely. She was now a person who knew that some things can be lost, and lost forever. For the first time, she understood that there is no "they" who can give back what we need or want. There's only us.

Our memories are always in pieces. We don't need the river Lethe for that. How many stories of my great-grandmother were lost in the decades before I lost that ring? Today, I know nothing of her but her name. There are no scraps of grocery lists bearing her handwriting, no diaries that contain her scribbled worried thoughts or tender dreams. We have forgotten names and faces, most of history, and fragments of our own pasts.

Still, death is something different in the Christian story than it is in the underworld of the ancient Greek imagination. While the river of forgetfulness dis-members us from ourselves and our stories, death in the Christian context re-members us—puts us back together. In this story, death is not a river where we forget or a land where we are lost, but a table where there is bread: a common-wealth where we are restored. Drink the river to forget; eat the bread and remember.

Jeff and I believed different things, but we had the same job. We both told ancient stories. We both woke them up, let them breathe again. There was life in the re-telling. That's what our demon friend, creeping up from the basement, caught us in the act of doing that night. Practicing our not-forgetting. Etching into memory the most important thing: that when we draw together around a table and break bread we are at once the most human we will ever be and the most divine. We have lost many things, but at this table we are here, and whole.

When St. Lydia's moved into 304 Bond Street, I felt this urge to understand the patch of land where our church made its home. I ordered books and did online research, matching street names to the stories I read. Before Dutch settlers landed on the island of Manhattan, the Gowanus was a green marshland, fed by a freshwater spring. The Gowanus Creek, as it came to be called, meandered through wetlands and ponds before making its way out to the sea.

The Lenape tribe lived along its banks. Then the settlers showed up and started building dams and digging out millponds, extending the canal and constraining its flow. Early letters from Dutch settlers refer to oysters "the size of dinner plates"[2] harvested from the estuary.

By the 1800s the creek had been dug out and widened into a canal and the nearby salt marshes drained. Its banks were steadily lined with tanneries and gas plants, the byproducts of which contributed to the now-murky water. By the middle of that century the canal was functionally an open sewer.[3]

We'll never get the Gowanus back. For decades it's been tied up in government squabbles about how to clean it up and who should cover the expense, but even after cleanup, it will never support plant life and wildlife in the way it once did. Walking by, you can smell the centuries of misuse. We can make affectionate jokes, call it "Venice" with air quotes implied. But the waterway is teeming with the chemical fallout of our sin: a constant reminder of the way we've dismembered creation. The creek is gone, and I sometimes wonder if we have nothing to show for ourselves as a culture but slime and toxicity left behind for the poor and cold, gleaming buildings rising up for the rich. Nothing but cranes and empty scaffolding, industrial tarps rattling loose in the wind.

I search, but can't find a single image of Gouwane, the Lenape chief after whom scholars believe the canal was named[4]. He doesn't appear in any land deeds of the 1600s, but he's thought to have owned a maize farm south of the Dutch settlement Breuckelen. We took his land and speak his name, but what about his face? Who was he and what did he see when the Dutch arrived, their eyes widening as they took in the fertile land, the estuary teeming with fish?

We don't need the river Lethe to forget. We do that all on our own.

That same autumn, as the demons rise from the basement, St. Lydia's observes All Saints' Sunday—a day dedicated to those who have died. At Dinner Church I hand out slips of paper the color of autumn leaves, and we write down the names of people we want to remember: a mother, a brother, a mentor, a friend. We hang the names from ribbons strung above the tables where we eat. The saints are with us but gone, remembered and forgotten.

"God remembers what we forget," I tell the congregation when I stand up to preach. I believe this means God remembers Gouwane, remembers him and the ones whose names we don't know—the children who played at his feet, the mother who bore him and nursed him. It means God remembers the name and face of every slave who built the city I now live in. God remembers those whose faces were never captured in photographs. God remembers for us.

Later that year, in the dark of a February night, I'll travel from one coast to the other after an interminable limbo in Newark Airport, waiting for the skies to clear in Canada. My mother has discovered a lump in her abdomen, a large mass lurking behind one of her kidneys. She showed the bump, pressing out through her belly, to a nurse friend of hers. Working to keep her voice calm, she instructed my mom to go immediately to the hospital. Now we are all waiting to see what it is, what it might be, what it might do to her. We know that it is huge, that it's been growing for a while, and that if it's in her kidney, it could be very bad.

I wait in the airport with the other stranded passengers, circling like a shark around the terminal, past the Hudson News and the Auntie Anne's pretzel place. We can't get out, and everyone has a rumpled, sodden look. Parents have relinquished their phones and iPads to their children, who are at this point wide eyed and hopped up on sugar or in various stages of meltdown.

My mom met with the specialist in Seattle today. She'll get the results of her scans while my plane flies through the dark. I won't hear the news until I've landed. When we finally board and push back from the gate, I listen to two podcasts and watch a movie, and I'm fine until we begin our descent toward the lights of the city. Then, the verdict is both too close and too far away at once, and I cannot stop myself from curling toward the window and sobbing into my sweatshirt. Spread out below us are tiny houses lined up in rows, lights glowing, private lives lived out at each address. I know in a different way now that my mom won't be here forever, and I pray a desperate, fevered prayer, *God please just give us a few more years.* There's too much I'll regret if we lose her now.

Finally on the ground, I fumble with my phone, trying to get a signal and read the email my dad's sent. The cancer, though advanced, is not renal cancer, and likely hasn't spread. I collapse back in my seat as the other passengers deplane around me.

In the terminal I feel light with relief. I wait for my luggage in a heady daze, a loose grin on my face even as tears leak down my cheeks. No one asks if I'm okay, and I'm glad. It's late and we are the only ones scattered through a deserted baggage claim, waiting for the small possessions we need to finally make our way home.

When I arrive, there is a tenderness in the house I've never experienced. A certain awareness of our fragility, unacknowledged until now. We treat each other like precious objects, like family relics nested in cotton that we must be careful not to lose or break.

Piled in a wooden chest are brittle books of photographs, sliding loose behind plastic sheets or slipping from their adhesive mounting corners. Ella. Dorothy. Ionne. They gaze out across decades, hair pinned high, dresses trimmed with knotted rosettes and lace pieces. And my great-grandmother Beatrice. Here she is with three little girls (my mother and her sisters) wearing saddle shoes and white socks with the cuffs folded down. They balance together on a beached piece of driftwood. Beatrice kept the primitive cabin where they spent summers fresh and clean with homemade curtains and sweet touches, like wildflowers in a vase, my mother told me.

In the photographs, she leans against a wagon-wheel gate and smiles, or dips the feet of a grandbaby into the waves on the shore. This is the same woman who will slip out of the house as she grieves the husband she loves and walk straight into Vancouver Bay. But here, in these pictures, she is young and smiling in a gingham dress and pearl earrings, as if nothing will ever change.

This will all come later. But tonight on the banks of the Gowanus, a block away from our church, Persephone, wearing a crown of wheat and roses, steps into the arms of Hermes, that cad who manages to tease from her a reluctant smile. The story has never been told quite this way before. Here on our canal we tell it anew, an ancient story rising up from the dust, taking on flesh and bone, reminding us what we believe or don't believe in. The pair dances together to a ragged waltz, under the polluted spill of streetlight. We lost souls float on our barge, atop centuries of refuse, the oil and shit of the dead slicked around us.

Charon, devoted but silent, looks on as the one he loves is pulled into the arms of another. We all have our jobs to do. Hers is to dance and his is to row. Ours is to watch, and we do, rocking gently on the foul water, the legacy of my ancestors, as the music plays and Persephone twirls in Hermes's arms, away from the gaze of a jealous king. This scene will never be played again—not just this way. We are the last to see it: the only ones who will remember this exact, particular moment. She must do this while she can, before she recedes for one more year to that place where all is lost.

III

JUSTICE

We will fight for you instead,
side by side with the others,
with everyone who knows hunger.
—PABLO NERUDA

Deep Waters

When the waters swell and pour over the walls of the canal, seeping up the streets and back alleyways, I am not there to witness it. At that exact moment, I'm probably dragging my mattress off the bed frame and shoving it close to the brick wall of my studio apartment, as far from the windows as I can get it. It's Monday, October 29. Hurricane Sandy is making landfall in New York City.

Outside my apartment, the wind has already picked up. Earlier that day, I checked the flood map the city circulated online, to be sure I don't need to evacuate. I'm safely in the green zone, but a block away, closer to the canal, the map is orange. The wind batters at the windows with a force that sets my heart racing, and I wonder if the mayor wasn't wrong. Maybe I should have sought higher ground.

I make my little nest on the floor, phone clutched in one hand, and tune in to NPR. Sitting alone in my apartment, Brian Lehrer's voice, familiar and sure, becomes a security blanket. He is there in the studio, into the darkest hours of the early morning, talking with New Yorkers over the phone with the compassion of a priest and the steadiness of an incantation. "You're out there, and we're not leaving. We'll be here all night," he says at one point, or at least that's the meaning I glean from his words. Though I'm sure he is surrounded by staff and producers, shuffling papers and wading through phone calls from listeners, I picture him alone in the studio, water rising steadily around the walls of his building.

Across the East River, sea water is pouring into the footprints of the Twin Towers, spilling through the unfinished museum floors set in their foundations. By 8:00 P.M. the MTA sends out a tweet that the subways are flooding too. The backup power at NYU Langone Medical Center has already gone out. Nurses heave critical patients onto stretchers, carrying them down fifteen flights of darkened stairs by the beams of flashlights to ambulances waiting below, red lights spiraling. They carry IVs behind them and pump respirators by hand. Just across the East River, water surges around the glass building that houses Jane's Carousel. Still lit, it's like a beacon in the darkness, horses frozen mid-prance, manes mid-toss. And in my corner of Brooklyn, the polluted waters of the Gowanus swell over their embankment and begin to creep across parking lots. One block west, water seeps into the basements of the Gowanus Houses, and the power snaps off.

All of this while I drift toward sleep to the sound of Brian Lehrer's voice on the radio.

Tucked among the reams of pages that make up the Bible, there is a story of a great flood. We often tell it to children. With its description of a towering, pitch-covered ark and an orderly procession of animals filing inside in pairs, the tale is both fantastical and comforting, despite an overtone of doom.

In the beginning, God's creation is a great project of categorization: creating an ordered world with fine lines drawn between light and darkness, land and water. God creates a place for everything: for animals to mate and birth and grow and gallop, for insects to creep and fish to spawn, for greenery to push out lush, thick growth. God's boundaries open up a space for life to proliferate.

But with the flood, creation is undone. God smudges her hand across the page and blurs away her own charcoal lines. She flings open the windows in the heavens, and the line between the sky and the earth is smeared. Water subsumes the earth. The tape runs backward, toward the void.

The reason for this destruction? Regret.

The text tells us that God regrets making the world because it has become so twisted—corrupt and filled with violence. I guess I can understand that. God crumples her paper, and humanity with it, then throws it away, missing the wastepaper basket. All but Noah, his family, and the floating menagerie he's sawed and hammered into being: a cacophony of brays and screeches, birdsongs and toad croaks. The ark is a microcosm of creation itself, floating upon the deep.

Noah must have been frightened. The great boat creaks and pitches in the storm. He wonders if his construction job will hold. His wife stares out at the water, which has swallowed everything they knew—the house where their children were birthed, the hearth where she cooked and daydreamed. It has swallowed their parents, their closest friends, the butcher she greeted each morning on the square, the blind woman who stood at the gates and begged. All the world's animals, snorting, stomping, and trumpeting, are a terrible kind of company when all you wish for are your friends.

When the waters recede, Noah and his wife find that they can see something they couldn't see before. They start again. Noah builds a new altar. God hangs a bow in the sky and vows that she will never again undo the world.

When the waters receded in New York City, we discovered parking lots of taxicabs floating in water and yachts strewn blocks from the shore. Our small section of the world had become disordered. Water isn't meant to flow up streets. Furniture isn't supposed to float in houses. Subway tunnels should not be awash with seaweed and starfish. Yet that night, they were. We, like Noah, could see something we couldn't see before. While some of us weathered the storm comfortable and safe, others were taken by it, and some just barely made it through. For many, there would be no recovery. In the wake of the storm, we saw it clearly: that some of us never had a chance.

In my nest on the floor, I awaken to a bright morning. The wind is gone, and the street eerily quiet. I flick the lights on and off. They're working, and the refrigerator is still cold. Outside, I bike the soggy streets, strewn with debris and branches. Ancient fallen trees are festooned with yellow caution tape, their roots tipped up, like posh ladies upended with their skirts around their waists. I feel I should avert my eyes. Lower Manhattan is entirely without power, they report on the news. So are Red Hook in Brooklyn and the Rockaways out on the beach—anywhere near the water.

That night I walk with friends to Atlantic Avenue, a busy four-lane thoroughfare that's usually dense with traffic. We stare out across the East River at the skyline of Manhattan, eerily dark and silent below Fourteenth Street, like somebody accidentally flipped off the light switch. Tonight, it's still a novelty.

Two days later it's Halloween. My friend Mark, who is without power at the Episcopal seminary in Chelsea, crosses the Brooklyn Bridge by bike (the subways are still down) to get a shower and charge his phone in my apartment. He tells me it's spooky in Lower Manhattan without the lights. We carve tiny pumpkins into jack-o'-lanterns and set them outside for what turns out to be a muted celebration of Halloween. Usually our block is the place to hit, a trove of well-prepared neighbors with good candy, but this year there are just a few trick-or-treaters, looking flattened and ghost-eyed, their parents worn and wrinkled.

It's becoming clear that this is a greater disaster than we imagined. Posts on social media have a panicked edge to them. Scrolling through, I see things aren't good in Red Hook; they're calling for volunteers. I bike past the genteel brownstones of Cobble Hill and under a highway overpass to volunteer at a Catholic church where the pews are heaped with clothing. It's hard to know how to help. There are piles and piles of comically unnecessary items—high heels and suit jackets—as if those weathering the storm are urgently preparing for a job interview. Jake came out to volunteer tonight too. Now he's around the corner wearing hip waders and bailing water out of someone's basement. Someone instructs me to sort clothes into heavy-duty trash bags, and I start in ineffectually, feeling certain everything will be unpacked and repacked in a different way tomorrow. Every contribution seems flaccid in the face of this great wall of damage, and I tamp down a rising sense of panic. There is too much lost, too much chaos to try to set it all right again.

"How are you?" I text Jake later that night.

"This is crazy," he writes back.

Four days in. I venture across the block to a community room at the Gowanus Houses, where piles of diapers and formula and bottled water are being sorted and stacked by residents. Facebook and Twitter are buzzing with needs in the neighborhood and how to fill them. "Diapers at the Gowanus Houses!" "Coats and blankets at Wyckoff Gardens!" Donations are coming in from people a few blocks away, or residents in the houses themselves. Volunteers line up and are handed clipboards and pens and dispatched.

I learn that when the basements of the houses flooded with water, it shorted out the electricity, which means no heat, no elevators, and no running water. A lot of the city's public housing units are in this situation. Their equipment is so out of date, left unmaintained, that the repairs are taking forever. The effort is entirely led by residents, supported by a Brooklyn organizing group called FUREE (Families United for Racial and Economic Equality). In the community room, a grandmother presides over the din from behind a folding table, shouting instructions. I can smell spaghetti and meatballs wafting through from the kitchen next door. I've heard the community room has been closed for years, caught up in bureaucratic red tape, but apparently the residents have taken charge, and it's open now, sanctioned or not. New infrastructure is designed based on necessity.

The woman behind a folding table pairs me with a lanky white guy with an earnest expression, gives us a handful of water bottles, and sends us to canvas the towers. We push tentatively through the front doors, unlocked because the electricity's out, and into a darkened, tiled lobby. Passing the silent elevators, we climb the stairs a flight at a time. It's daytime, but the windows are narrow and the hallways are dim. They smell like abandonment. Many people have left to stay in hotels or with family, but those who can't are still here. We knock on the doors one at a time and wait for answers. The sound of shuffling inside. The door opens, chain still drawn across the gap. A father stands with a child at his feet.

"I'm fine," he tells us, "but check on Ms. Turner in 265. She needs diabetes medication every day." We mark this all down on our clipboard. It seems unbelievable that no one else has taken charge of these efforts—just residents struggling along. But residents are the only ones here.

At the end of my shift I pick up groceries for dinner at the corner store, just like it's an ordinary day. Commuters are perusing the vegetable section, deciding on a head of broccoli or a bag of snap peas. But a few blocks away at the houses, an elderly resident is sitting in the dark and the cold, in danger. The dissonance is impossible to reconcile; it short-circuits something in my heart. I go home, put water on to boil for dinner, start crying as I'm chopping carrots. The storm has revealed something I didn't want to see.

Days later and the subways still aren't up. People wait in hours-long lines for gasoline. There is desperation in our eyes. *Are we okay? Is this okay?* Still, my apartment is warm and dry. I spend an entire day trying to figure out how to get a can of gas to a Lutheran church member in Howard Beach whose generator has gone out. I can stand in line for gas, and my colleague Ben has someone who can drive it to her, but we can't find a gas can to carry it in. They're backordered for days. Simple things have become impossible now.

The Church of St. Luke and St. Matthew has been commandeered by a group of activists who cut their teeth at Occupy Wall Street. They've reconfigured as Occupy Sandy and set up shop in the Clinton Hill sanctuary. I lock my bike outside and push through the heavy church doors to a hive of activity. Someone has taped a torn scrap of paper to the baptismal font that reads, simply, "Donations." There's a coms unit in the balcony where scruffy kids in knit caps sit in the glow of laptops populating Google spreadsheets. Down below, the pews are filled with cardboard boxes coming in by delivery from around the county, sorted and sent out to affected areas. Everyone has a Sharpie in their pocket and a roll of duct tape on hand.

It is beautiful to see, this spontaneous organism of organization, lurching forward and developing systems and processes on the spot. Its goal: to bring relief to people who are alone. I hear things I'm not sure I believe: our volunteers are getting to people who haven't been reached by the cops or emergency response teams. Someone found a dead body in a tower in Coney Island.

I'm not the only one feeling overwhelmed. At church on Sunday night my congregants report feeling shaken. At the end of service, we gather around the Christ Candle, sleeves rolled up from doing dishes. I make announcements as the offering plate goes around.

"There's volunteers needed every day at the Gowanus Houses," I tell them, "and over at St. Luke and St. Matthew with the Occupy Sandy folks. But listen. Be gentle with yourselves. This . . . has us all shaken up. Just take things one step at a time."

"Thanks," Hannah says after church, flipping her long hair behind her shoulders. "I've been feeling so strange and it's so surreal. I feel like I should always be helping, but I'm also really tired. Every day is so up in the air."

Congregants volunteer around the city, after work and on weekends. The days are patchy and episodic. We're playing each day by ear, plans changing at the last minute based on which trains are running. Jake and I both pitch in at Occupy Sandy, but he's out canvassing while I'm at the church doing trainings. Everything feels fragmented. Every day is piled with contingencies. If the F is on a limited schedule, Hannah will go to work, but only if the A is running below Fourteenth Street, and if it isn't she'll try to meet me to volunteer.

On Sunday, we come back together to the strong tables at church and affirm that God is still in the heavens, even if our world feels upside down.

When I was a kid, my mom told me that if I was in trouble, all I had to do was call 911, and everything would be fine. I believed her: that if someone just knew you were at risk, the benevolent forces of the world would conspire to keep you safe. To a child like me, that seemed like the end of the story.

Then, in my twenties, I watched as we abandoned the city of New Orleans to Hurricane Katrina, elders and poor folk, mostly African American, crammed into the Superdome without dignity or basic living conditions. I saw for the first time that being rescued depended on being valued by the powers that be, and being valued had a strong correlation with being wealthy or white.

With Sandy I saw it again, but this time, uncomfortably close up. It was the poor neighborhoods where the power remained off for weeks and seniors languished without medication. The projects had been built in the forgotten places, on the edges of canals like the Gowanus or out in Red Hook, where the subways don't reach. We put them there because it was cheap, left them unmaintained because it was cheaper. When the storm finally came, the folks who lived there didn't have the cash to shell out for a hotel room or miss work for a week, so they stayed. We couldn't fix things fast enough because everything was too broken to begin with.

Power was out at the Gowanus Houses for eleven days. Living that long without power might have been sustainable in a house or a suburban neighborhood, but fifteen flights of stairs and no elevator made those dangerous days for the elderly and disabled. After Halloween, a snowstorm blew in. With the heat still out, residents were left with no sources of warmth but their gas ovens. Parents (already negotiating ten flights of stairs with babies and toddlers in tow) kept their kids home from school, embarrassed they couldn't bathe. The power came back on November 9—then, two days later, a water main broke, and eight of the fourteen towers were again without running water. Right across the street in my row house apartment, I had heat, electricity, and all the water I would ever need.

One hundred seventeen people died because of that hurricane. Forty of them drowned in their homes, deaths which the CDC noted, in their report of 2013, should have been preventable. Red Cross volunteers collected reasons why the deceased who lived in evacuation zones did not leave their homes, presumably from living relatives. The reasons included "afraid of looters," "thought Hurricane Irene was mild," and "unable to leave because did not have transportation."

In those weeks, I see things that leave me shaken. Children in New York City without drinking water. Volunteers who discovered dead bodies. Walls imbued with black mold, and elevators left dangling on the fourteenth floor. Like Noah after the flood, I can see something I couldn't see before. My eyes are wide open. Now it is impossible to close them, and my heart feels like it's tearing in two.

We've been shattered. But there are moments of communion.

With the power still off in Red Hook, a local church starts hosting a spaghetti supper every evening so residents can come and get a hot meal. One of those evenings, the Rude Mechanical Orchestra is invited to come and play dinner music. Someone thought it might cheer things up. We arrive at the church with our padded cases slung over our shoulders and make our way to a basement fellowship hall, where big pots of sauce are simmering on the eight-burner stove.

As residents trickle in, we play a few tunes, picking out the least aggressive of our protest songs. After a while we run out and slide into old hymns. "Just a Closer Walk with Thee," "Amazing Grace," and "This Little Light of Mine." The residents seem suspicious of us young newcomers but after a few bars decide to reluctantly tap their feet or nod their heads as they wait in line.

After playing a set or two, we sit down to our own spaghetti supper. The line for dinner has tapered off, but it's still early, and we've only played for an hour or so.

"Let's go out on the streets," someone suggests. We're

a marching band, after all. And so we hoist our horns and plunge out into the night toward the Red Hook towers. The streets are wide and empty; without power, there is no comforting glow of streetlights to mark the way. The neighborhood is still and silent as a tomb, and the towers loom in front of us, every window dark. We process onto the pavement courtyard at the base of the apartments. It's like standing at the bottom of a canyon.

It's deathly quiet. I wonder if we should really pierce the night with the sounds of brass and drums. We don't live here. Is it an intrusion?

But the bandleader is already counting us in on a tune and I take a raking breath, pushing out a ragged line with the tubas that rips open the night. The drums snap in, laying down a beat, and the trumpets blare out a reply to our low brass call. We're off and running, playing a version of the "Internationale," tricked out with a beat. It's a song that's been sung for workers' rights for a hundred years, by the French Workers' Party Choir in 1888 and the protesters at Tiananmen Square in 1989. Our rendition smacks off the brick buildings, ricocheting back, as if we're entirely alone. Fingers dance on valves. We hit the chorus and loop back into the verse.

And then.

High above us at a window, a flashlight appears. A lone circle of light shines down. Then the flashlight begins to bounce. It's moving, I realize, in time to the music. Soon another light blinks on, followed closely by another, illuminating in each window like lightning bugs on a summer night. Behind each flashlight is an unseen face. Kids and parents, grandmas and uncles. Windows slide open, and claps and hollers come cascading down to us.

There in the Red Hook Houses, an impromptu dance party takes place, spanning four buildings and fourteen floors. Down in the courtyard, our band plays and dances, in joyful communion with the souls above us. We're belting out the melody and it rebounds off the brick, reverberating its way to the top of the towers, launching toward the sky above. Our multi-building dance party is pure joy in the face of destruction. I think that we are reminding one another of something we can't forget: that even in the face of injustice, the floodwaters will subside, the night will not last forever, the days will grow longer, even if the worst is yet to come.

With each line of harmony, I'm trying to say something to my neighbors. The message, encoded in bass line and drumbeat, is sent out like Morse-code dots and dashes shot through the expanse of space.

You've been abandoned. It was wrong, I want to say. *No one should weather the storm alone.*

Good Fridays

Kneeling, I unroll a sheet of brown wrapping paper on the floor and weight the corners down with a couple of Bibles. With a pencil, I sketch out the words "Black Lives Matter" across the top in big block letters. Then I start googling.

Two weeks ago Michael Brown was shot by the police on a hot August day in Ferguson, Missouri. I watched an interview with his mother and couldn't bear it. That Sunday after Dinner Church, our little congregation filed out onto the sidewalk in front of 304 Bond Street holding lit candles and signs for Michael Brown. Singing, we walked in procession up to Smith Street, met by the stares of diners at sidewalk cafés, forks suspended mid-bite. Then we curled around the corner past the Gowanus Houses. One resident lifted his fist in solidarity as he crossed the street. Others ignored us.

Our small act of remembrance didn't feel like much in the face of an overwhelming problem. A dozen of us, walking along, singing. But I needed to do something. I needed to say no with my body, and I guessed that my congregants needed it too. For four weeks, after Sunday night Dinner Church, we sang and walked, knowing that more work was coming.

I want to connect young Michael's death to our own city's legacy of police violence—to show that this is a systemic problem, not an isolated incident. So, my computer in my lap, I research Black and brown people in New York City killed by the police. It's a harrowing exercise. Some names I recognize. I write down "Amadou Diallo," and his age, twenty-three, shot in 1999, on my length of brown paper. I was in college that year and only vaguely aware of his story. I read about the forty-one shots fired and the nineteen that hit. About the square wallet Diallo took from his pocket the police assumed (or later claimed they thought) was a gun. One of the officers involved, Kenneth Boss, had shot and killed an unarmed Black man two years earlier. But thirteen years after Diallo died, the same officer earned his firearms rights back. In 2015, he was granted a promotion.

I inscribe "Ramarley Graham" on the brown paper; he was the eighteen-year-old whom police sighted leaving a bodega in the Bronx in 2012, adjusting the waistband of his pants. Later, after they followed him home (they said he ran, but video footage shows him walking), Graham's grandmother let the cops right into the apartment when they knocked on the door. They tore through the place and found Graham in the bathroom. There, Officer Richard Haste shot him once in the chest and killed him. They later said he was trying to flush a bag of marijuana down the toilet.

I write down the name of Kimani Gray, who was only sixteen. I write down the name of Sean Bell, killed with fifty shots fired at him and his friends at his bachelor party. He was supposed to get married the next day.

I write down every name in pencil on my sheet of brown paper, the corners fighting to curl up. One of the names is Nicholas. A boy who was only thirteen when he was shot by police in 1994, I read. And then I frown. Nicholas Naquan Heyward, Jr., was killed in the Gowanus Houses, just yards away from where I sit in my apartment.

I remember a mural I've seen on a wall, somewhere in the neighborhood. A smiling young boy beams out at the viewer, wearing a graduation cap. Doves hover on either side of him, and he holds a scroll: *In Loving Memory*.

When I type Nicholas's name into the search field, the site for a memorial foundation pops up. There in the center of the front page is Nicholas, smiling brightly in a red graduation gown and tie, proudly holding his certificate of graduation from junior high, this look in his eyes that says, "I did it."

Nicholas, I read, was playing with a friend in the stairwell of the Gowanus Houses. The two were playing cops and robbers with an orange-capped toy gun when a cop came across him there and lifted his gun—a real one. Nicholas's friends reported that the child raised his hands. "We were only playing," they heard him call out. The police officer, Brian George, shot him in the stomach. Taken to a Manhattan hospital rather than a closer one in Brooklyn, Nicholas died eight hours later.

I write Nicholas's name on my sign. His age, thirteen. The year, 1994. I am careful to space the letters evenly. The sign begins to feel like a prayer, every name inscribed in pencil and then carefully traced again in black marker. I finish tracing the last date and then sit down in an armchair and start to cry.

The next day, Julia and I hang the sign on the inside of St. Lydia's storefront window.

"I hope no one throws a brick at it," I tell her.

It feels presumptuous to place these names in our window. The phrase "Black Lives Matter" feels uncomfortable on my lips, not because I don't believe it to be true, but because I know how terribly far I am from my life not mattering. My life has always mattered: to my teachers, my principal, to the cop who smiled at me as I jaywalked across the street with friends. I could have been holding a real gun, and he would have coaxed it out of my hands.

Sitting at a desk at St. Lydia's, I watch passersby slow down to read the sign. Some of them pause their conversations mid-stride, while others stop to read carefully. One afternoon, a family hovers there for more than the usual few moments. I pop my head outside, and they say, "Nicholas Naquan. We knew him. We remember him."

I don't remember Nicholas. But the people who do—who read his name at the window—seem to walk away just a tiny bit lighter. Maybe it feels good to know that someone else is trying to remember too. His community made a mural to remember him, and someone who's not part of his community, but who cares, took a permanent marker and wrote down his name, and hung it in the window.

The first time I preach about race at St. Lydia's, I tell a story from third grade, when my father came to visit my classroom. My teacher, a plump, smiling white woman who favored lacy blouses and calf-length floral skirts, stood with her back to us, writing up multiplication tables on the blackboard. She led us through them one by one, calling on students for the answers.

Some, like me, sat with our hands raised high, confident that two times two equaled four. Others slumped at their desks with their heads propped up on a fist. She called on them too. But my dad noticed that she never called on the Black students, who made up a third of our class. With each equation, kids' hands would shoot up in the air, but my teacher would point to only me or Shawn or one of the Jennifers. It wasn't that the Black students received no attention at all—she'd chastise them to sit up straighter and stop fidgeting. I don't remember at what point in the year they stopped raising their hands, but I'm sure it didn't take long.

By the time I reached sixth grade, I looked around my honors English class and wondered why, when so many

Black kids attended our school, there were only two in my honors classes. One of them was Lamar Franklin. With round reading glasses, a bright smile, and an endearing gap between his front teeth, he was a charming kid, well liked by everyone. Lamar persevered through teachers who wouldn't call on him and principals who spoke to him only to tell him to pull up his pants. But many others didn't. My public school was enacting the school-to-prison pipeline. I saw it play out right in front of me, but never knew it had a name.

I tell the congregation this story.

"What kinds of lessons do you think I learned?" I ask them. What assumptions did I inherit about who was smart and who wasn't, who was good and who wasn't, who was of value and who wasn't?

All those lessons, never explicitly taught but implicitly enforced, were engraved in my subconscious. Sitting at my desk with my pencil box and blue-lined paper in front of me, I learned an unspoken curriculum. I memorized the order of the planets and the life cycle of the butterfly that year, and soaked up the quotidian qualities of ordinary, small-town, run-of-the-mill racism.

I am shaking as I speak.

The Lydians sit, nodding and wide eyed. Perhaps they are sifting through stories of their own—remembering the advantages or disadvantages they received.

After church, I go home and basically curl into a ball, feeling vulnerable and exposed. Words and I have never exactly gotten along. When I was a kid, talking to grown-ups or teachers, my words always seemed to get tangled up. I felt as if I was fighting a battle against chaos, trying to get them to line up the same way, always ending up tripping over them and blushing in class.

When I reached divinity school, words had me convinced I could never be a pastor. I showed no promise in public speaking; my professor remarked in my evaluation that I seemed "constantly surprised to find myself preaching." Things did not improve as St. Lydia's was getting started. Each Sunday night those first few years I would offer my sermon, rigidly reading from the pages I had written, never improvising.

Standing up to preach has meant acquainting myself with a certain feeling of dread. Now, wading into preaching about racial injustice means acquainting myself with the suffering of the world and allowing it to do its work on me. My words aren't always graceful or eloquent. They lack the practiced flourishes of my divinity school colleagues. Instead, I figure the best thing I can do is just point to what I see, and hope others see it too. Just uncover the truth we've all been avoiding.

I have learned to wrestle with words. Some things are too important not to name.

A month later, I attend a community meeting about rezoning in our neighborhood. I notice that while the public housing residents, almost all of darker skin, are given a chance to speak at the microphone, their comments never seem to catch hold. The conversation just slides back to the concerns of the wealthier, whiter neighbors, armed with Ivy League vocabularies and a sheen of entitlement. I watch what amounts to a small uprising of housing residents who live in the flood zone of the canal, complaining that after a storm their tap water turns brown. Their council member thanks them for their comments and moves on.

"How do you think this process is going?" I ask him after the meeting. I'm wearing my clergy collar, and it lends me a kind of moral authority.

"I'm very pleased," he says. "There's always a diversity of opinion, but we're moving forward together."

"These people don't feel heard," I tell him.

That same summer, I watch grainy cellphone footage of a two-hundred-pound cop throwing a fifteen-year-old Black girl to the ground and kneeling on top of her. Her name is Dajerria Becton, and this video of her assault at a Texas pool party has gone viral. The officer, Eric Casebolt, is twice her size and armed with a nightstick and a gun. Her body, lanky and insubstantial, clothed only in a bikini, seems so slight and exposed under his weight. He sits down hard on her back and shoves her face into the ground with his hand, shouting, "On your face, on your face."

It is difficult to imagine that this slip of a girl could possibly be a threat. All she can say is "Call my mama," over and over again.

The video of Dajerria Becton is not the only grainy cellphone footage we see in that season. I listen to the cries of Freddie Gray in Baltimore, placed in the back of a van requesting medical aid he never receives. Then he dies. In

June, Dylann Roof walks into a church in Charleston and sits with the Rev. Clementa Pinckney as he leads Wednesday night Bible study.

Roof waits for them to begin praying before opening fire. In my third-grade classroom, the little girl next to me holds her hand as high as mine, smiles, and waits to hear her name. *I have the answer,* she's thinking, but no one calls on her. "I can't breathe," he's saying, but no one listens. "Don't shoot," he tells them, and holds up his hands: they are empty.

Church folk often say that God "uses your weakness, not your strength." I never really understood that idea. It doesn't seem like an effective strategy.

But I learn the hard way that those church folk are on the mark. Each time I stand up to preach on race, I am flooded with a spectrum of unpleasant emotions, from low-grade dread to full-fledged terror, a tangled disaster of raw nerves and vulnerability. My biggest fear is that I will fail to get this right, and let down the few Black folks who are part of our congregation.

"Well, she tried," I imagine them saying to themselves after service, "but she really doesn't get it." Shame and humiliation are high on the list of how this can all pan out. Addressing racism in my preaching asks me to lay down the notion that I am some kind of an expert.

"Learning in public," Jake says to me over glasses of iced tea in a corner café in Brooklyn. Ever the big brother to me, Jake has been a conversation partner as the church has embarked on racial justice work. "You're not going to get it all right. But that doesn't mean you shouldn't do it. The congregation's going to watch you learn. And they'll learn too."

Walking home, I turn over his words. If the biggest thing I have to risk is being embarrassed, I need to get over it, because at risk for Black folks are their lives. I really don't want to get this wrong. Not because I need to be perfect, but because I'm a liability.[1] White folks trying to do justice work tend to be filled with need—to be one of the "good ones," to be praised by the people we say we're showing up for, to take the lead when we should be following. It's not just annoying, it's damaging. And I don't want to do damage.

There is this uneasy feeling that I can so easily drift away: recede into the soft cavern of safety that is available to me at any time. I can step into the fight for justice, but just as easily step out, while the people across the street have no such option. I will never experience their particular set of harsh realities.

My granddad didn't graduate from high school, but he worked his way to the engineering department at Memphis Light, Gas and Water—a position unavailable to his Black compatriots. The red lines drawn on city maps kept him in, not out,[2] so with his higher earnings, he was able to buy a house that gained value. When my father was born, my granddad could count on him attending decent (fully segregated) public schools. Their family was poor, but my father was able to excel and earn a full-ride scholarship to Yale. Only a hint of a southern accent and the lack of cash in his pocket kept him from camouflaging himself alongside the kids from Park Avenue and the legacy students.

The forces that lined up to bring my family from subsistence farming in rural Mississippi to the middle class were myriad. In two generations we accrued education, property, and wealth, never available to the Black kids who grew up in Memphis. And now here I am, always with an exit.

But I want to "dismantle the legacy of my forefathers," as my friend Lenny, an author and activist, once told me.[3] I want to know the stories of my past and our neighborhood. I want to know our neighbors, to see St. Lydia's become a part of these blocks. After the hurricane, I can't just stay on my side of the street. It hurts to think of how alone we were.

A flyer changes everything. Just one sheet of eight-and-a-half-by-eleven paper stapled to a telephone pole.

For years I've been steadily trying to build relationships in our neighborhood, but they seem to slip through my fingers like sand. I've attended community meetings, asked for one-on-ones with leaders of local organizations. There are emails back and forth, cancellations and re-scheduling. One organization is going through a change in executive directors; another's leaders are all chronically overworked. Some don't work with religious groups.

The Gowanus Houses seem like an impenetrable fortress. I know there have to be community leaders who live there, but I'm flummoxed when it comes to connecting. I've made sheepish phone calls to the Gowanus Houses Residents' Council and left messages, but never heard back. Phone calls themselves are bad enough—waiting with anxiety for someone to pick up, breathing a sigh of relief when no one does, and then fumbling my way through a message. But I also feel the pressure of being misread: another white girl who thinks she can "make a difference," dripping with privilege, deigning to stoop for a moment toward a neighborhood she'll abandon when things got too hard. I'm different from that girl, I think. But then I wonder how.

Then: the flyer. Walking home from St. Lydia's to eat dinner between meetings, I notice a colorful sheet on a telephone pole. "Gowanus Houses Arts Collective," it says. Kids can come this summer to learn about photography, make films, mix music. There's no website, but there is a Facebook page. At home I study the page like a scholar examining ancient runes. Excavating my way through the links, I dig up a video posted on YouTube by a kid who lives in the houses. He's walking around the neighborhood, talking about growing up there and all the ways it's changing. I type out a message and hit return. This time, I hear back—from Tracey.

A week later, I'm sitting across from Ms. Tracey Pinkard in the residents' council meeting room in the basement of the houses. We're in wheeled chairs situated around a board table. At the back of the room there's a metal desk scattered with papers. A phone blinks with messages, its spiral cord curled up in knots.

Tracey has a demurring manner and a kind smile, but a sharp, discerning eye. Steady and gracious, she tells me about the arts collective she and Chris (the filmmaker behind the lens of the video I saw) are starting up. I can see she's assessing my intentions. *If people are coming in,* she tells me years later, *are they saying we need to be fixed or saved?*

Tracey leads me down the hall to a room she and Chris have transformed into an art and music studio. Kids' paintings are pinned up on clotheslines to dry, with their splotches and swipes of primary colors. Yogurt containers are packed with paintbrushes, bristles pointed to the ceiling.

"You may remember in last year's participatory budget process, the Gowanus Houses won money to reopen our community center," she tells me. I nod. I had followed the residents' efforts. The community center had been closed for years—residents made unsanctioned use of it during the hurricane.

"The money still hasn't been released," Tracey tells me. "But I want the kids to have a space. So we're down here for now." She casts her gaze across the room. Coils of hair falling around her face, she has a broad, smooth forehead and soft eyes. "I don't want them to lose their faith," she says.

I invite Tracey to speak at St. Lydia's. I ask her to tell us stories of the neighborhood she grew up in, and where she sees God at work. She stands under the gaze of attentive Lydians and holds up a picture of her grandmother Ms. Hazel Tyre.

Tracey's grandmother (or Mrs. Thelma, as many of her neighbors called her) moved into the Gowanus Houses in 1947 and lived there for twenty-one years. She always kept her door open. She knew every kid's name. She grabbed them by the elbow and asked them how school was going, kept an eye on them.

"I just try to wake up and do God's will," Tracey says. "I'm in a unique position because of the way my grandmother raised us."

Tracey grew up in the houses and moved out, never planning on coming back. But when her grandmother died, the apartment in the Gowanus Houses was open to her. She had her own children now, and a job working with high schoolers at Brooklyn Collaborative school. When she moved back, she felt her grandmother's presence inviting her to step into her role.

"My neighbors are proud, skillful, and talented people,"

she tells us at Dinner Church. "And we are all exposed to repeated trauma. Poor housing conditions, police brutality, gentrification. Because of this, our resiliency coexists with apathy. But take Hurricane Sandy. Our community comes together to make things happen for one another."

Tracey serves as vice president of the residents' council and cofounded the Gowanus Houses Arts Collective. She's always working to connect the houses to resources and bring residents together. She shows up at meetings. All while raising her own children and working at a local school. I see Tracey as an educator and activist, a fighter and a matriarch. I see her as a spiritual guide: someone who sees the truth and lives life from a deep well of down-to-earth integrity. But when I ask Tracey to describe who she is, she says she's not any of those things. She says, "I'm just . . . being a vessel. Just someone who really cares."

Over at the arts collective, a group of Lydian congregants join the residents who volunteer, helping the kids make potato stamps or batik fabric. Charlotte goofs off with the kids, joking around as they dip their stamps in paint, letting them draw a blue stripe down her nose.

Every fall there's an Open Studios weekend in Gowanus, when working art studios across the neighborhood open their doors to the public. The event draws visitors from all around the city, and Tracey and Chris and I start thinking it would be incredible for the kids from the arts collective to show their work. We ask if we can host a community exhibit—photographs of the neighborhood by the kids who live here, taken as part of a class Chris ran in the spring. We call it Perspectives: Youth Reflections of Gowanus.

Chris picks out the best photographs, and I bike to IKEA and return with fourteen white frames stuffed in my saddlebags. A congregant who's a curator gets everything hung on the walls in our narrow storefront. Each photographer writes a short statement about their work.

On the day of the show, a cadre of grandmas arrive, pulling grocery carts packed with big tin trays of rice and beans and chicken wings and jugs of juice. They sit at our tables fanning themselves as visitors start to trickle through the doors. Tracey, I find out later, called just about everyone she knows in the houses.

"You have to come and see the kids' work," she told them. "It's just down Bond Street."

Parents from the houses poke their heads in tentatively.

"This is the right place!" I tell them, ushering them inside. They look around the room to find their kid's name, and beam at the photograph on the wall.

"Our Jerome, he took this!" a father says proudly.

Weaving around the grown-ups are the artists themselves. Eight or nine or twelve years old, they're busy handing out flyers and tying balloons outside to show where the exhibit is.

One of the younger girls, Sydney, took a photograph of her friend on a swing in motion. "I started by trying to capture my friend on the swing," she wrote in her artist statement, "but she was swinging too high and fast and that's when I noticed the girl waiting in the middle of all this movement. I know that feeling of having to be still when you don't want to be."

Sydney stands in front of her piece, chest puffed out and beaming, talking to an art student about her photograph. He asks her some questions about the lens she used and smiles at her answer. I meet a batch of new people: a sculptor with red-framed glasses whose studio is a few blocks over, a family who just moved into a brownstone down the block, a pair of community organizers, and a filmmaker. Some of them have lived here for years and didn't know the Gowanus Houses existed.

One photograph, by fourteen-year-old Ethan, gives me a pang to look at. It shows barbed wire in the foreground, brick towers out of focus in the background.

"I live on the thirteenth floor in the middle of the Gowanus Houses," he writes. "When I'm there I'm always surrounded by larger buildings and don't think of it as part of a larger neighborhood. The barbed wire feels to me like how Gowanus is separated from Carroll Gardens. It's sharp, almost cut off, despite the fact that it's just a short walk from here."

Outside the windows, Ula's Access-A-Ride is just pulling up. I smile to myself. In the early years, Ula drove me to distraction with her sharp jabs and sarcastic comments. But we've settled into a begrudging regard for one another. She often gives me a hard time, asking me obscure academic questions she must know I won't be able to answer.

"I thought you'd know your Christian history better after all that education," she gibes.

I roll my eyes at her. "Ula, I didn't do a PhD on the Reformation, okay? Let me research it and get back to you."

Over at the tables, the grandmothers offer a heaping plate of chicken wings to the sculptor from the other side of the canal. She sits down next to them to trade stories about the neighborhood back in the seventies. "Nope, you didn't cross Court Street," I hear one of them saying. "Not if you didn't want to pay for it," and they all crow with laughter. A couple Lydians are learning the names of the young photographer's family who just arrived, smiling and showing them the way over to their child's photo. Across the room, Sydney gives a balloon to a toddler in a stroller who moments ago was wailing. "Do you like orange, or white?" she asks. The toddler points mutely to orange and reaches out to clutch the curled ribbon with her chubby hand, letting loose a delighted laugh.

I feel sure my heart is going to brim over. Neighbors are meeting neighbors they might never have thought to talk to. We're all around one table, scooping up rice and beans and sipping Capri Suns. *The kingdom of heaven*, I keep thinking. At least, for just this moment, we're all around one table.

Tracey tells me that Mr. Heyward holds a Day of Remembrance for his son every August. She says I should go. And so, on a broiling summer Saturday, I don a clergy collar and a sleeveless shirt and walk half a block to the park that bears Nicholas's name. The older kids are on the basketball court, the younger kids shouting from the sidelines or chasing each other across the park, faces sticky, smeared with red Popsicle. I'm not sure what to do with myself. I don't see Tracey or anyone else I've met at community meetings. I settle on an awkward white-lady-lurking posture, trying to smile in a friendly but not invasive way.

Mr. Heyward is talking to the press over near Wyckoff Street. Soon he moves toward a podium and a press conference begins. He recounts the story of what happened to his son, holding up a plastic toy gun with an orange cap. A tall, slight man in a bright polo shirt and a baseball cap, he's been retelling this story since the nineties, seeking justice for the child he lost.

Halfway through the speech, his voice cracks and he places a hand over his eyes. His wife rests a hand on his shoulder and we all stand quietly, shifting our weight from foot to foot and fanning ourselves with our programs as he gathers the resolve to continue.

"Take your time," someone calls out.

Clustered around Mr. Heyward are several other families whose children or relatives were killed by police. The sister of Akai Gurley, shot in the Pink Houses in East New York, is there to speak. The father of a little girl named Briana Ojeda says a few words as well. She died in the car as her mother tried to race her to the hospital during an asthma attack, when a cop pulled her over and started writing her a ticket. "She needs CPR," her mother was screaming. "Do you know CPR?" The officer refused to call an ambulance as he wrote her a summons.

I realize that I've seen Briana's face before, and a chill passes through me. On my walk to the subway, there's a house I've always wondered about. Candles in glass holders are perennially lit in the front garden; there's a tree decorated with ornaments that say "angel"; the front door is adorned with a picture of a little girl. Now I know why. Her parents have been keeping vigil since 2010. Our neighborhood is dense with stories like these.

After the press conference I introduce myself to Mr. Heyward.

"I'm a pastor of a church just down on Bond Street," I tell him.

"Oh, that's nice, that's nice," he says to me vaguely, shaking my hand, before being pulled away by a reporter who wants a quote. I sense a pall of exhaustion hanging around him. His skin is drawn, his eyes weary. He's been doing this work for two decades.

At Dinner Church the next day, I preach about young Nicholas and his activist father. I tell the Lydians the story of how Nicholas died, and the room grows quiet. Wendy, her offering of home-baked dark chocolate–macadamia nut bars sitting on the counter, is here with Peter. As she listens to the story about Nicholas, she pulls him closer, wrapping her arms around him protectively, and setting her chin on top of his red hair. I tell the congregation about the work Mr. Heyward is doing to try to get his son's case reopened. Nicholas would have been our neighbor, were he still alive. His father is our neighbor. He lives just four blocks away, but it's like we're in different cities. Our kids are safe. His aren't.

At least now, we know his story.

These relationships with our neighbors took years to form. Even before we arrived at Bond Street, I taught congregants how to do one-on-ones with community leaders. We held a Season of Listening each spring and invited longtime residents to come and preach. We heard from Raymond, who came of age in the Gowanus Houses in the seventies, and fell in love with a Puerto Rican woman from the other side of the neighborhood. And we heard from Neil, whose parents and grandparents had all been baptized, married, and buried in St. Agnes Church on the corner. He painted a picture of life in the close-knit Irish Catholic community he grew up in.

These connections were good. We were meeting people and listening to the stories they shared with us, learning the history of the blocks where our church was situated, and coming to understand the unique pressures our neighbors faced. Every new connection was like a seed planted. Some of them sprouted and grew, but a lot of them just lay in the ground, dormant. Maybe the season wasn't right.

Maybe they'd come up later, when the conditions had changed.

But then we met Tracey, and overnight, a mess of vines sprouted and then flowered. A few seasons later, we harvested a bumper crop. Our friendship with Tracey was the right seed, planted in the right soil, at the right time. Something growing that wasn't there before.

Through all of it, I had no idea what I was doing. I was just casting out seeds and hoping something might happen. I felt lost and awkward a lot of the time. It would have been easier to stay in the walls of our little church, risking nothing. But I needed to catch hold of the ropes, pull our small wooden boats together. I needed us to be at one table. And maybe all those Sunday nights of practice—sitting at tables with people we barely knew and trying to make conversation—prepared us in some way. We cultivated a new spiritual practice: a tolerance for discomfort and ambiguity. We learned how to reach for one another, even when the gulf seemed wide.

You know that I was lonely through all of it. Searching for someone whose eyes would light up when they saw me, who would take my hand. I was hungry for love. But buried deep at the bottom of that aching hunger was a different kind of desire. A longing that was rooted not in the absence of a partner, but in the devastation of the world. My salvation came through rice and beans served up from foil trays and passed from hand to hand.

A year later, and it's time to celebrate Nicholas's birthday again. I head across the street on another hot August day, but this time I'm not all by myself. I announced the celebration at St. Lydia's and asked the congregants to come with me. Mr. Heyward has invited us to set up a table, and it's there that I meet Wendy and Peter. Phil is there too, carrying the St. Lydia's banner and our welcome book. Earlier this summer at the St. Lydia's retreat, he and Wendy confessed that they were a couple, to the hoots and hollers and cheers of the entire congregation. Now they're engaged, and Phil is slowly becoming a dad to Peter. We get the table all set up together, struggling to tape everything down so it won't fly away in the hot wind.

Peter is twelve. His hair is just as blazing red as it was last year, and his pale face is scattered with freckles. He watches the other kids on the basketball court, none of them white like him, and sticks shyly to our table before making friends with some girls who grab his hand and run to line up for ice cream. They are just about the age Nicholas was when he died.

This year the program is different. As we all sit crosslegged on the asphalt, Mr. Heyward tells us he wants to let Nicholas speak this year, in his own voice. He reads from an essay Nicholas wrote when he was eleven.

"The reason why I picked my nature name to be Nicholas Newt," Mr. Heyward reads, "is because a newt and I both have similarities. For example, I am rarely seen by people, mainly because I tend to spend my school days and weekends home . . . I am also a good swimmer because of my quick legs just like newts are quick swimmers because of their flattened tails."

We all smile the way you do when a kid is sweet and smart and funny, except this kid isn't around anymore. Then Mr. Heyward reads from a letter Nicholas wrote when he was ten:

Dear Malcolm X,

My name is Nicholas Heyward. I am 10 years old and I live in Brooklyn New York. I admire you a great deal because you taught Black people to be more politically aware and to stand up for their civil rights. And to choose their own destiny. You also stressed that education and political power is necessary to accomplish these goals. I also admire the organization you called the Black Coalition which went to Black communities, teaching them equality and justice for all people and the importance of sticking together with words of nonviolence.

Mr. X, I believe that I have good qualities such as a standing up for my rights when I am wronged. And I also like to read. I think reading enhances the intelligence.

Yours truly, Nicholas Heyward

Those were summers of death. We watched name after name become a hashtag on the national stage, while across the block, our congregation learned the story of Nicholas.

They were also summers of beauty: of astonishing things revealed when those who refused to be voiceless waged their revolutions. I was made breathless by the images of Bree Newsome scaling the flagpole in front of the South Carolina capitol building, suspended high in the air, the Confederate flag stripped of its power in her victorious hands. The following year Corey Menafee, a dishwasher at Yale's Calhoun College, reached up with a broomstick and smashed a stained-glass window depicting two slaves weighed down with loads of cotton. "That thing's coming down today," he recalled thinking. "I'm tired of it." He tapped it twice and out it popped, falling from its frame and shattering to pieces on the sidewalk. He was later led out of the dining hall in handcuffs and stripped of his job.

Their acts were hard-won and came with immense risk. Imprisonment and legal fees. Loss of job and income.

Perhaps we all reach a moment in life when we're given the chance to shatter the death-dealing constraints clamped on ourselves or others. When, despite the relentless grind of dehumanizing limitations, we rise, breaking windows and scaling flagpoles, showing everyone who witnesses our ascent that there's a different way. The photographs capture only the climax: a window shattered, a flag in a woman's fist. But they do not reveal the fear, trepidation, and uncertainty that qualify the time before and after. The tedium of planning, the infighting among allies, the terror of yielding yourself and your body to handcuffs and prison and the mercy of a network of judges and lawyers for whom you are only a name on a list.

These moments are racked with the daily hopes and fears that every life is burdened with, made up of seconds ticking by and small decisions made, premeditated or on impulse. Anyone who's ever done anything extraordinary is ordinary. But when the moment comes, they say yes, and God's realm comes beaming through.

You only get there by acknowledging the truth. I grieved through those summers. I always imagined that I earned everything I had in life, through smarts or hard work or perseverance. Turns out I'd just had a lighter workload all along.

Christians have a season for truth telling. It's called Lent, and it's a time for repentance, which sounds scary, but really just means "turn around." Rooted in the story of Jesus' forty days in the desert, fasting and praying, Christians sometimes give up chocolate or meat in Lent—some small thing that might seem inconsequential in comparison to the ills of the world. The minute practices, though, point to something bigger—the ways we use sweets or alcohol or overeating or undereating or Netflix bingeing to help us avoid the truth.

Turn around: away from whatever you're drawn to that's trying to kill you. From the distractions that keep you from feeling the grief of the loss you've endured. Turn around and see the truth: that the Confederate flag must come down. That the stained-glass window must be broken. That even though you believed you loved all your third graders equally, and treated them equally, you were wrong.

Each week after the sermon at St. Lydia's, I hand out slips of gray paper and each person writes down a truth they want to confess. We spend some time doing this. Then we sing a song about the grace God offers—*here is forgiveness, full and free*—and hang the slips of paper from bare winter branches we've installed on the ceiling.

At the end of Lent we arrive at Good Friday, the day that Jesus was hung on the cross. For our worship service, I create stations around the room. At each one, there's a large photograph in a frame, and candles to light. Congregants make their way from station to station, kneeling or writing, sitting silently with eyes closed, praying.

The photographs are historical and contemporary. They point not to our individual sins—the lie we shouldn't have told, or that we drank too much and raised our voice at our spouse the other night—but to what Christians are really talking about when we talk about sin: collective sin. The tragedy of how, simply by living in this world, we take part in a system that is inherently broken—racked with social ills like racism and poverty that we participate in every day.

We stand in front of *The Soiling of Old Glory,* a photograph of a white man in a rage holding an American flag, moving to strike an African American man with it. Beneath the photo, there's a caption: "They shouted, 'Crucify him! Crucify him!'" And then, "Pray for communities that turn into crowds."

There's the image of David Kirby, dying from AIDS with his partner at his side. This was the shot that finally awakened the nation when it appeared in *Life* magazine in 1990, rousing us from the Reagan-induced denial of an epidemic that had already taken thousands of lives. "They kept coming up to him, saying, 'Hail, King of the Jews' and striking him on the face," the caption reads. And then a confession: "We have allowed those who are suffering to be ignored, mocked, and brutalized."

There is an image of a young woman in Baltimore. Seen from behind, her hands are held up—a mirror of Michael Brown's "Don't shoot"—strong and brave, as she is faced down by a phalanx of police in identical riot gear. She is unarmed, unarmored, and alone. "Then Pilate took Jesus and had him flogged" the caption reads. "Pray for those who are victims of violence at the hands of the powerful."

With the irony that is indicative of the Gospel, redemption starts not with self-improvement, but by looking straight at the most broken, twisted part of ourselves and simply saying, "I'm a mess." What a relief, to remember that we can't fix ourselves on our own. That, in fact, we're not even fixable—but, impossibly, we are loved.

There are tears, clasped hands. Time slides by, and I wonder how we can persevere, this tattered human family of love and cruelty and despair. Then we begin to sing. We lift the portraits from their places and bring them outside to our pocket-size garden, unfinished and pockmarked, a little like us. The aluminum fence posts make the figure of a cross, and we lay the photographs at its base, along with the candle we light every week to represent Christ, nestled in a wooden bowl. We pile our prayers in front of the cross. Then I invite us to make our confession.

There is silence. And then there is truth.

"I confess that I keep myself walled off from my family because I'm afraid they might see me for who I am," someone says.

"I confess that I use work as a convenient excuse to avoid intimacy."

"I confess that I don't want to feel the pain of the world, and so I try to ignore it."

"I confess that I treat some people like they're worth less than others, even though that's not who I want to be."

"I confess that I'm afraid that I'm too small."

It goes on for a long time.

"I confess that I think I can do everything on my own," I say without lifting my head. Something unclasps around my heart. It feels good to stop struggling, and just tell the truth. A soft place opens in me. I can see where I've fucked up without feeling like I'm going to die. I've inherited elitism, passed on to me through education. I pass certain people over, without even realizing it. It's not pretty to look at. But if everything doesn't depend on me being perfect, I'm free to be opened, and to learn. Confession won't solve all the ills of the world, but I wonder if it's the only place to start.

Then I tell the story of how they hung Jesus on the tree to die and how the land was dark and the curtain in the temple tore in two. Hannah and I kneel on the ground and blow out each candle, one by one. She's so gentle, you'd think she's blowing an eyelash from the face of a baby.

Down the block, Nicholas's father grieves.

Across the country, Michael's mother grieves.

Sandra.

Eric.

Freddie.

Who is my neighbor?

We were only playing, he called out before the cop pulled the trigger.

I blow out the Christ Candle.

Nicholas.

Another life gone.

EMPTY TOMBS

S tanding on the subway, wedged between a tiny woman's overflowing grocery cart and a Hasidic man reading an impeccably folded newspaper, I read a chilling story
in *The New Yorker* about a man named Antonio.[4]

"You just need so many things to actually ride out the
apocalypse," Antonio is quoted as saying. A forty-year-old
and former Facebook product manager, he recently purchased five acres on a small island in the Pacific North-
west. There, he built a house, outfitting it with generators,
solar panels, and thousands of rounds of ammunition.

Antonio is a prepper, someone who's actively making
plans for mass societal chaos brought on by natural or
man-made disaster. According to the article, making arrangements for the collapse of society has become fairly

common. People like him purchase property in remote places, keep their families' bags packed, and plan to jet away to an isolated paradise on a moment's notice as the world topples behind them.

While people from any economic bracket can go a little overboard stocking canned goods in the basement or building bunkers out back, prepper culture, I read, is taking the 1 percent by storm. There is a growing awareness among billionaires that economic inequity could put them in a pretty awkward situation should resources ever become scarce. "The fears vary," the article says, "but many worry that, as artificial intelligence takes away a growing share of jobs, there will be a backlash against Silicon Valley, America's second-highest concentration of wealth." So they're making an escape plan, protecting themselves from the angry, hungry mobs who might one day appear at their doors.

The article describes a fifteen-story luxury apartment complex in Wichita, Kansas, built underground in a disused missile silo. Finished in 2012, the place has a lounge with a large stone fireplace, a gym, a pool, and a medical and dental facility. In the absence of windows, LED screens in each room broadcast a live feed of the prairie outside. You can change channels to display an image of a forest or a city. Outside the silo, armed guards stand watch. Apartments in this complex sold for three million dollars each.

Rattling along on the 2 train, I start to feel queasy. The idea of ultrarich people making incredibly expensive provisions for themselves, and themselves only, when they are the very people who have the capacity to address the world's need, is ironic. Not to mention that such wealth is often built on the impoverishment of the rest of the world. One critic wrote of the prepping trend, "Why do people who are envied for being so powerful appear to be so afraid?"[5] We all have our preferred ways of managing fear, and there's nothing wrong with self-preservation. But living fifteen stories underground, with armed guards under orders to shoot your fellow human beings should they approach, watching the live feed of a prairie you'll never actually see . . . Is that life?

To me, it sounds suspiciously like a tomb.

In a few days, St. Lydia's will celebrate the Easter Vigil. We observe Easter not on Sunday morning, but on Saturday night, enacting a liturgy that's been passed down through the ages. After the hollow ache of Good Friday, we'll wait on Saturday for the sun to go down, gather on the sidewalk, and light a fire. The "new fire," it's called in our tradition. I will fuss over it, mixing Epsom salts and alcohol that will ignite when a match is lit—a little stagecraft that makes the night more dramatic. Then we'll light the Christ Candle from the fire and stand around it as I sing ancient words to a melody that a friend composed for us. He always accompanies me darkly on the accordion. "How holy is this night," I'll sing, "when wickedness is put to flight, and sin is washed away. It restores innocence to the fallen, and joy to those who mourn." Every year my voice catches on those words, "joy to those who mourn."

This idea of a movement from brokenness to fullness—
that even from the shards of the very worst of human violence, God can make something whole—brings tears to
my eyes.

At this year's vigil, we will read the resurrection story
from the Gospel of Luke. Women come to the tomb
early in the morning to anoint Jesus' body, but when they
crouch down to enter, they find it empty. They're standing there bewildered when two men appear beside them
out of nowhere, saying, "Why do you search for the living
among the dead?"

The Easter Vigil is the fulcrum of the year at St.
Lydia's—our most extravagant celebration, with drinking
and dancing well into the night. "This is the night," I will
sing, echoing words passed down through the centuries,
"when wickedness is put to flight and sin is washed away."
Everything lost will be restored. The last few years, an
awareness of the world's brokenness has erupted into my
life. I've seen what's left after the storm. I know Nicholas's
story. Ula's situation is growing worse each day as she
bounces from one bad nursing home to the next, caught in
a dearth of resources. I am still lonely. But God is making
life, even at the tomb.

The writers of the Gospels, it occurs to me, were living in
a prepper's worst nightmare. Forty years after Jesus' death,
Christians had formed fragile, new communities, many of
which existed under the shadow of violent persecution.
In Judea, tensions between the Jewish people and their

Roman occupiers boiled over into revolt. By A.D. 70, the city of Jerusalem was taken in a violent siege in which the Jewish people were slaughtered and enslaved. The temple—God's dwelling place and the heart of Jewish life—was set on fire and fell. For Jews and Christians in the region, life was overcome with destruction. The fabric of their society hung in shreds.

They had a choice. They could hunker down, find the first-century version of a bunker, and hide their families deep underground. Instead, they did something different. As the world was rent apart, they came together around a table to share a meal. At the center of their community, they placed a story of death and life.

They remembered another day when everything was wrong—when the land went dark and the curtain in the temple was torn, and humanity turned into a vicious crowd and hung God on a cross to die. At the center of the story are the women who awoke before dawn, moving through darkness carrying jars of oil, their bodies aching, the memories of that trauma-laced Friday still invading their thoughts like sudden screams as they went to prepare their friend for burial. But when they arrived at the place of death, they found not a body, but a pair of angels as fleeting and transcendent as lightning.

You're searching for the living among the dead, the angels told them, and sent the women out on the road, back to the disciples, to be disbelieved and ignored.

Years later, the Christians who gathered in the wake of their own ruin and destruction told this story of violence and execution, of missing corpses and fractured community. When everything was in tatters, they spoke of life that comes from death.

This, too, is the story we choose to tell, standing in our own ruined city. It is a story that does not offer one shred of security. We will not hide away in fear, building walls to divide ourselves from our neighbors, hoarding what we have. We turn and reach out toward the world, still trembling, to encounter a living God who longs for us to be one family and will not be bound by death.

We all spend our fair share of time hanging around tombs. It's a pretty normal, human thing to do. Death seems to draw us back like a lure.

My personal tomb has the word "perfection" written across the top. I hover at its edge, thinking I can control things, thinking I can do it all on my own. Thinking that if I can't, I probably shouldn't even try. So I stay locked on the edge of death, paralyzed.

Why do you look for the living among the dead? the angel asks me.

"Listen, I've got it under control," I answer.

I was your classic overachiever. I have a vivid memory of the first time I got an answer wrong in the first grade. Mrs. Levitsky called on me, told me, "No, that's not it," and moved on to the next student. I sat in my kid-size chair, bathing in shame. If my answer was wrong, *I* must be wrong too. But if I found a way to please everyone, 100 percent of the time, then everything that felt like it was falling apart would hold together, just barely. So my hand shot up in class, and my tests were returned with A's. I smiled and learned to please.

In the early days of St. Lydia's, I needed every sermon to be inspiring, every song to be exactly right. We were building a church on the conviction that mistakes and brokenness are where God enters in—I must have thought that applied to everyone but me.

"Emily," I remember Ana, a mentor, saying to me over the phone, "let God do the heavy lifting."

It sounded like a foreign language. I was the one who was supposed to be doing the lifting. That's how I'd know I was worth something.

I've got it under control.

Then my mom got sick, and I didn't have it under control at all. There was nothing I could do to achieve my way through this situation. No way I could work harder to change her outcome. Then the hurricane hit, and I didn't have it under control. Then Trump got elected. Then your sister was deported. Then the cops shot your son, your daughter, and didn't even get taken off payroll. Then the rent gets raised or the job falls through. Then the sky goes dark and the fabric of life is rent in two. Around you, the city is falling.

On those Good Fridays, it is God, not we, who stitches us back together. And God offers not a bunker that will provide imagined safety, but a road to walk: uncertain and exposed. Grace shows up, not in the ways we try to hold it together, but when we finally let go.

Why do you look for the living among the dead? the angels ask.

We come together in a church basement whose concrete columns have been painted a thousand times with high-gloss paint. Last time it was a clergy breakfast at 10:00 A.M. with untouched platters of elaborate pastries (everyone's trying to eat just a little better). There are paper cups of coffee from urns, a portable screen teetering on skinny tripod legs, and a projector plugged into coiled yards of a Day-Glo orange extension cord. There are PowerPoint presentations with arrows and pie graphs, flip charts and dried-out markers.

This is a meeting of Faith in New York, a community-organizing coalition of over seventy congregations in the city. Over the last few months the Lydians and I have become fixtures at these church-basement meetings. Hannah, Jason, Malika, and I all trudge to the subway at the end of the workday to ride for an hour to Ozone Park or Bay Ridge. There we attend the Prophetic Leadership School, soaking up the basics of organizing as we scratch notes on pads of yellow legal paper. We sit while the leader's words are translated from Spanish phrase by phrase, a room of one hundred church folk waiting patiently even though we're moving at half time, nodding in understanding and support.

Faith in New York is led by Onleilove Alston.

"My name is Only-love—that's right, my parents named me a phrase," she always jokes when she introduces herself to a group, her broad smile manifesting, bringing a glint to her eyes beneath the African-print head wrap she often wears. "People always ask me if they were hippies or if it means something. Well, in African culture, you usually name a child based on the circumstances of their birth or on a characteristic you see in them."

The first woman to lead Faith in New York, Onleilove laughs often but makes light of little. Though she stands a full head shorter than most of the male pastors she leads, her authority is palpable as she walks us through area median income calculations and the fight for affordable housing in our city.

Onleilove started organizing because she experienced firsthand the consequences of bad policy. As a kid, her family became homeless when her stepfather lost his job. She was placed in the foster-care system because of a now-defunct law that allowed kids to be taken from homeless mothers. Today, she will settle only for a world in which every child and grown-up is given the best possible chance.

Advancing the slide on her presentation, Onleilove is strong and sure as iron. She knows the Bible backward and forward and, without flinching, names the work our communities have to do. Catholics need to do more to support undocumented folks who attend and advocate for so many of their churches. Black men experience oppression but also must examine their misogyny. She rejects false dichotomies with a deft hand. There is not either/or with Onleilove, only a clear call toward what is right.

She listens to each of us with unblinking attention. Even the rumpled man with a stack of flyers he's eager to hand out who always stands on the fringes of the meetings, waiting for his chance to elucidate the evils of capitalism. He's not wrong, but he does tend to go on for a while. She gives him honor and respect, and pulls a gem of wisdom from his tumble of words, even as the meeting risks running overtime. Everyone has a voice at the table she lays.

I am a lover of beauty. I revel in placing flowers beside the Christ Candle at St. Lydia's and smoothing bright cloths on our welcome table. Church basements like these are not usually thought of as beautiful. But between paneled ceilings and linoleum floor, in our Faith in New York meetings I start to see beauty of a different kind, illuminated by compact fluorescent lighting. The paint is sometimes peeling from the walls, but the will of the people is strong and their prayers are earnest and true. The desire to understand one another—to honor each other with full attention—is rare and extraordinary.

We pray together often. Sometimes we are invited to reach out and touch the shoulder of our neighbor so that Hannah and Jason and I are linked together with the pastor from the Baptist church in Queens and the Puerto Rican lay leader from Washington Heights. Some of us wear collars and some suits, some pray in the name of Jesus and say, "Father, we just ask that . . ." and others read from a prayer book tucked in their breast pocket or their purse.

I am one of the youngest clergy, and I wear my collar to make sure no one mistakes me for an intern. But I don't feel like a rare bird here. I feel like we're all rare birds, milling together and just noticing that each of us has wings. No one expected us to flock together—undocumented immigrants and Ivy League graduates, Baptist preachers descended from sharecroppers, Catholic Sunday school teachers, and a former foster kid from East New York. But here we all are, together, catching a glimpse of a different kind of world we could create. Maybe this is my flock.

I watch the election results come in at a bar up the street crowded with Brooklynites, with Julia. The night starts out cheery enough, but then Florida goes red. When Pennsylvania follows, the mood in the room shifts, as if the hair on everyone's arms has raised at the same time. A hush falls over the crowd as the newscasters glance offscreen, looking for answers.

I order steak frites and a cocktail, then devour the medium-rare cut mechanically, as if applying myself to stress eating will change the results. It doesn't.

People start posting on the St. Lydia's Facebook group, "What is happening??"

"I don't know, but I'm praying," I write back.

By this time the entire restaurant is silent and stunned.

Tears are running down one woman's cheeks. Julia is aghast, her head leaning on one hand, as if to shield her eyes. When the results start to seem final, I post that the church will be open the next morning at eight. At home, I stay up until three watching the broadcast. I sleep fitfully, shock like caffeine in my veins. At six I lie awake. I shower and go to the church, and find the door unlocked. Omar is inside sitting at the table. They got off the night shift at five at the clothing store where they stock shelves and didn't know what else to do, so they came here.

"Let's order breakfast," I declare.

"That sounds good," Omar says, dazed.

Omar is new to St. Lydia's. Young, just twenty, with a loose, four-inch afro and always stylishly dressed, Omar has also recently decamped from a giant megachurch.

"I went to their huge training program in Australia," Omar told me their first night at Dinner Church, eyes wide, "but it turns out I'm *totally* gay. The staff had me talk to this chaplain, but she wasn't really into conversion therapy, so I was lucky. Anyway, now I'm back in the Bronx living with my parents and I have no idea what to do with my life because all my friends are in college."

"Holy crap," I said.

Omar jumped right into St. Lydia's and became fast friends with Hannah. In a few years Omar would shift to using they/them pronouns, to better express their gender identity. They'd also nurture an interest in fashion and the environment that they would follow to art school. But the morning after the election, Omar, who is usually hilarious and giddy, is devastated.

"We live in public housing," Omar tells me. "You think Trump's gonna help my family?"

We set up a prayer area at the front of the church near the benches, with tissues and candles to light. All day long congregants and random people who heard we were open stop by. They come over for little stints to talk in spurts with us.

"I have Obamacare," someone says.

"My father is undocumented," someone says.

"They've elected my abuser," a woman says. "He told the whole nation that he grabs women whenever he wants and they elected him."

"Will my marriage still be legal?" someone asks.

Not everyone is shocked. I, and many of my congregants, have led lives in which the system mostly worked for us. We feel betrayed by a nation that would elect a man who's such an enormous fuck-you to Queer people, trans people, Black and brown people, refugees, Muslims, and women. But many of my colleagues of color do not need to wrestle with shock. They knew what our nation was long before I awoke to the new, naked reality. They have always been the subjects of betrayal.

The Faith in New York meeting just after the election is packed to the gills. There are a crop of new, frazzled white folks with dull shock in their eyes, trying to figure out what to do. But the women who work between shifts for the rights of immigrants and the undocumented, the Black pastors who have fought to ban the box so the formerly incarcerated have a chance at a job—they are not surprised. They've seen this all before.

We do our work from a basement, but we will not hover by the tomb. We divide into teams and get to work.

Through the wash of bleak winter days when facing the "new" reality seems all I can bear, Faith in New York decides to plan a week of action. The mayor keeps calling New York a sanctuary city, a place that will "resist" Trump's agenda through noncooperation. But kids still get stop-and-frisked on the street, and Muslim leaders are being surveilled. The city is not a sanctuary for them.

We plan five demonstrations, one for each day of the week, culminating in a "Sanctuary Art Build" in front of the mayor's house on the last day. Maya, an organizer, is heading things up. There are planning meetings, trainings, phone calls—so many phone calls dialing in a meeting number and pass code. I receive text after text from the organizers, filter all the information back to the Lydians so we can all participate.

On Tuesday we hold a press conference to kick off the week. On Wednesday a procession of mourners holding cardboard tombstones that say "R.I.P. Affordable Housing" glumly loops around the hotel where the New York Board of Realtors is holding its annual luncheon, as my friends from the Rude Mechanical Orchestra play a funeral march. Later in the week, folks descend on the offices of City Council members for a "pray-in," to encourage them to push for legislation that prevents police brutality.

Thursday, a group of Lydians, bundled in coats and scarves and brandishing signs, arrives at Washington Square Park, where we join ranks with a hundred Faith in New Yorkers gathered there to protest the wrongful deportations of our undocumented neighbors. I'm edgy and nervous. We've planned for civil disobedience, and I've never been arrested before. To make things more complicated, I started my period yesterday. We're not supposed to be in jail that long, but right before we start marching I dash into a corner restaurant and change my tampon, hoping it will hold out.

Then we're off, with a chant and a drumbeat. We march west through the Village toward an ICE building on Varick Street, in Lower Manhattan. A number of our protesters are undocumented; for them, an arrest would have grave consequences. They, along with others, push together on the sidewalk, into a cordoned off area, shouting, "Sanctuary now!"

I move toward the street and take the hand of an Episcopal priest I know from Brooklyn. The light turns red, the cars pause at the intersection, and twenty-seven of us, clasped together, wade out into the street and form a chain across the thoroughfare. The goal is to block traffic in front of the building that hears cases and serves as a temporary detention center. Bridging the distance from sidewalk to sidewalk, we stand firm. The traffic light changes, and horns begin to blare.

The police are already waiting there, because this is what's called a "planned arrest." The lights bear down on us. From behind me I can still here the chants of Jason,

Omar, and Hannah, along with the others, urging us on. The cops are filming, and the news is there too. For some reason the police are pulling the taxicabs closer to us. I'm squeezing the hand of the woman next to me, whose name I don't know, a cardboard sign hung around my neck.

Taxi drivers start getting out of their cabs as the traffic builds up behind them, cars piling in and bearing down on their horns. They're all shouting, not for us to move, but for sanctuary. "Sanctuary now!" They join their voices with the protesters', raising their fists.

The arrest itself is slow and painstaking. An officer moves down the line, assigning a cop to each protester. My hands are pulled behind my back without force by a female police officer who stands with me as we line up for the bus.

Ahead, I see Onleilove being searched, and my heart lurches. I don't like to see her body in the possession of these officers. It is not a game or a stunt, a Black woman in the hold of the police, locked up.

We're loaded onto buses and crawl through city traffic, sitting uncomfortably on our zip-tied hands. At the jail, we're processed and then walked down a narrow cinder-block hall, small cells for four lined up to our left. We're exhausted, but over on the women's side, as each new protester is walked back, a heady joy rises up. We give a raucous cheer, clapping and celebrating for each arrival. We are jubilant because we choose to be. Our joy is the best defense in the face of death-dealing systems. We can't see each other, impeded by the cell walls, but we can shout one another's names and trade stories. After a while we start singing.

Onleilove is in the cell next to me, and we grab hands through the bars. She jokes that we look like a photo shoot for a diversity ad, and we laugh, loopy from lack of sleep. Later I sit and listen to the stories of a veteran protester in my cell, who schools me in the art of disarming authority. When the cops come by, they ask her citizenship. "I'm not answering that," she says mildly. They move on to the next question. "Authority often exists because we give it away," she explains. "Depending on our privilege, we can practice taking it back."

The cell is painted a sort of butter yellow, with a long metal shelf that can be a bench or a bed. In the center of the back wall sits a shining metal toilet. There's no partition, and the cops have removed all our personal items from us. As the hours go by and it gets on toward two or three in the morning, I start to worry I'll bleed through my tampon. We weren't expecting to be held this long.

Past three they come and unlock us using oversize skeleton keys that look like they're from a cartoon, hanging on a massive brass ring. When I ask the cop on the way out if I can use the bathroom, she asks insistently why I didn't use the one in my cell.

"Because I'm having my period," I tell her bluntly, "and I didn't want to take my tampon out in front of everyone."

"You can't use ours," she snaps. Access to sanitary items is limited if you're a woman in prison. I was in jail just overnight, with the assurance I'd be out in the morning.

But women in state prisons often pay five dollars for two tampons. They're sometimes forced to use socks or tissues. Jail is designed to humiliate: to strip away dignity and remind imprisoned people that they are without liberty.

There are some who would argue that we accomplished nothing that night. We blocked a street for a few hours, they'd say, maybe got a little bit of publicity. I would argue that our week of actions not only reminded our representatives that we are here, we are organized, and we vote, but accomplished something more. Placing our bodies in the way of life-as-usual, using it to stop traffic, to say no to an inhumane practice that should not be . . . reminded me, and all of us who stood together, that life can look a different way. The "world-as-it-is," as activists call it,[6] is rife with possibility. It's ready to break open into the world-as-it-should-be. Part of crossing over the barrier is acting like we're already there.

This is why protesting and working for change are not the only practices of revolution. We must dance, sing, cook, eat, and meet one another in love. Many call it foolishness, but we are cracking open the tomb and letting God's world break in.

Why do you look for the living among the dead?

Centuries ago, Christian communities stood in the rubble of their city and chose a story: of a day when the world ends and two grief-stricken women go out in search of the friend they love and return terrified and full of truth, with their hands empty. This was the choice they made: not to seal themselves in a tomb of despair and isolation, buried deep under the earth, but to break bread.

It's a brave choice. And one that takes place only when we're linked with our neighbors. Only a community of love will pull us back from the edges of the tomb.

"It's you," I preached to my Lydians at the Easter Vigil that year, "who are my living proof of the resurrection. You remind me what it means to live as people of love, right in the middle of this ruined city."

None of us can do this on our own. The mountains may fall and the stones may tumble, but we will only tell the story again.

IV

RESURRECTION

Love lives again, that with the dead has been;
Love is come again like wheat arising green.

—JOHN M. C. CRUM

BROKEN BREAD

Sunday night after church, Alicia hands me the keys to her beat-up Honda Civic.

"Anything I need to know?" I ask her.

"It has a CD player," she says, raising her eyebrows at the ancient technology. "And I called the insurance company and had you put on there. In the glove box there's a file folder with all the numbers you might need."

Alicia is more organized than one might assume. In cutoffs and a tank top with a blue streak through her dark hair and eye makeup that glitters faintly, she doesn't scream "Type A." But it turns out she's the kind of person who kits out her car with a filing system. She winds her fingers through those of her girlfriend, who's talking to someone next to us.

"I can't thank you enough," I say, hugging her.

"No big deal. I won't have to worry about alternate-side parking for five weeks!"

In my seventh year at St. Lydia's, I've started to get tired.

It's a wearing, aching kind of tired that keeps me in bed longer than I should stay there in the mornings. At work I stare at my computer screen, wondering blankly what exactly it was I was just trying to do.

Our building's physical needs are grinding. In the winter, the person hired to shovel when it snows doesn't show. Then the oven starts turning off mid-bake, throwing our volunteer cooks into a tizzy. Last week, the neighbors who live upstairs came down and yelled at me on the sidewalk during our midweek concert series. They don't like the noise, I get it. There is staff to help: Julia, who's part-time; Leah from England, who's become a part of the team; and interns who have joined us for the year. Even so, there is always too much to do and not enough time to do it.

St. Lydia's has many things: enthusiastic supporters and donors, priests and pastors scattered around the country who love the project and helped it get off the ground. We have mentors. We even have fans: a steady stream of churchy visitors who come to learn about a new way of worship. We're also a small, new church in a larger denomination, which can be rife with politics and institutional discord. While our relationship with our synod* had

---

*That's Lutheran-speak for a regional grouping of churches.

been strong for years, now it's strained. I whack away at bureaucratic red tape as if I'm trailblazing through a thicket, brandishing a machete. Every direction I turn, there's a new set of obstacles, a new fight waiting.

I feel like I'm dragging a net that's twisted around my ankle, gathering odd bits of debris. It's not a good way to lead a church or be a pastor. I am short-tempered and irritable, on the verge of snapping at staff, or even congregants. I'm *on my last nerve,* as my mom would put it.

"You need a break," Mieke tells me over pastries one day.

"I can't afford one," I say.

She shrugs her shoulders. "You need one."

We've met up at the Cornelia Street Café, our usual spot, to commiserate on a rainy Saturday. A few years ago, Mieke started up a congregation of her own—a quirky church that meets monthly, emphasizing musical improvisation and creativity. She and I have endured the trials of community making together.

"It's not like there are any nice retired ladies who come in on Thursday to fold the bulletins or organize the basement," I tell her, stirring a frothy hot chocolate. "These are young people. Everybody's always scrambling to pay their rent. The whole congregation's just trying to make it through."

"It's a city of hustle," Mieke offers. "Nobody has a lot of free time. I can barely get my people to volunteer for basic roles."

"I guess this is what happens when your church is filled with artists and actors."

Mieke nods and leans in. "My last service, the communion server got sick, the musician got a gig he had to take, and then my reader bailed at the last minute because she had a Tinder date." She pauses to roll her eyes. "So then it's just me, scrambling around trying to make everything happen. I can't do all the things!" She takes a decisive bite of croissant, for emphasis.

The rain falls lightly on the roof. Outside, a man scurries by under an umbrella, a bouquet of bright blooms wrapped in paper tucked under his arm.

"It's rough," I say. We pause, ruminating.

"I think the time's coming," I tell her.

"What, to leave?" Mieke is incredulous, her eyes huge.

"Yeah," I say, watching the man with flowers until he disappears around the corner. "It's not just the burnout. I'm feeling this tug. Like they're headed one direction, and I need to go another. It's not dramatic or anything . . . I just have this feeling that it's time."

"That's huge," Mieke says. "I've only ever known you as the pastor of St. Lydia's. Who will you be without them?"

"I have no idea," I tell her. My eyes fill with tears and I look away.

I take Mieke's advice, planning five weeks of sabbatical in the gray days of March and April. I scrape together money I shouldn't spend and rent a room in Asheville, North Carolina, with a claw-foot bathtub and crisp linens on the bed. I sublet my apartment to a couple from Australia who have just relocated to New York. Alicia hands me her car keys.

The next day, I'm speeding toward the Verrazzano Bridge, leaving behind the grime and grind, the tritone chords of taxi horns, the whoosh of the subway arriving in the station and repeated announcements to *stand clear of the closing doors.* A mixed CD a high school friend made me in 2004 blares from the tinny, rattling speakers. I'm euphoric, dizzy with this unburdening. I'm not responsible for keeping something afloat, at least not for five weeks, which feels like an eternity. I am weightless.

In Asheville, I climb mountains. I stuff a daypack with granola bars and an extra layer and follow a map up into the hills. I walk until the light changes and the sun starts to go down. It's scary to hike alone. I imagine twisting my foot on a rock and tumbling down the trail, ending up critically injured without cell service until nightfall, when coyotes feast on my flesh. But this never happens.

In the rambling Victorian house where I've rented a studio, I sleep until I wake up, and then write in a journal, cross-legged on the sofa, with a cup of milky tea. I take long walks through town. I spend four days sleeping in a bamboo shelter by a river in the woods, at a retreat center run by a guy who believes himself to be an elf. (But that's another story.)

I decide I want to learn something new, so I take weekly lessons in horse riding. My teacher, a solid woman with loose, wavy hair and a southern drawl, shows me how to approach the horse. She tells me I have a calm way with them and teaches me to find the horse's rhythm and move in tandem with it. My horse's name is Angel. She's white with brown speckles and has soft, beautiful eyes. Mounted in the saddle, I spend most of our lessons attempting to urge her into motion. Angel, however, is disinterested in trotting. She stands, unbothered, flicking flies with her tail. I enjoy the rhythm of brushing her down after our lesson, standing close to the heat of her body.

I go to restaurants alone and read *The New Yorker* at the bar with a coffee or a beer, unabashed and uninterested in attracting anyone's attention. I have been teaching myself to travel alone for years, and this trip is like the final exam.

In New York, I've been single for what feels like an eternity. It, too, is grinding. Now in my late thirties, I've reached a new, horrific stage in which I am ignored by men my age, who would rather date younger models. In Asheville, though, it turns out my dating profile draws just a little more attention. People write me, and I write them back. I go on dates—a lot of them.

One evening I'm getting ready for one of those dates with a mustached anarchist. I go to the closet to change into something more presentable and feminine. All week I've been hiking and horseback riding and wearing nothing but beat-up jeans and T-shirts. I take a skirt out of the closet and hold it up. Unexpectedly, a feeling of revulsion rolls through me. I put it back.

If he likes me, he'll like me like this, I think. I smooth on some lip gloss with my finger, and that's it.

It turned out he liked me like that.

I hadn't known it was possible.

I start to shed my skin. I slough off layers of bad dates and rejection, guys who never called back or physically recoiled from me when I uttered the word "pastor." I shed expectations about how pretty I need to be. I shed the idea that no one will want me if I don't pluck my eyebrows, fit into a size six, or laugh and smile and look through my lashes when he explains things to me I already understand. In a town where I know just a handful of friends of friends, I let the layers fall away.

I don't think I ever put on a dress again.

Right in the middle of the biblical library is the Song of Songs: the great love poem of our sacred texts. It tells a story about sexuality different from what most folks are taught in their junior high confirmation classes. Reading it, you might notice that the voice that opens and concludes the song is the voice of a woman, and her voice and perspective are dominant throughout the poem.[1] Second, this woman speaks clearly of her own desire, and openly communicates her plans to gratify it. In fact, scholar Cheryl Exum writes that "there is no other female character in the Bible whom we get to know so well through her intimate and innermost thoughts and feelings."[2] Third, we notice that the woman in this poem calls herself "black and beautiful," a fact that she says draws derision from other women. Fourth, this love poem is not about marriage. It's fairly clear that the lovers involved are not married,[3] and it is never mentioned that they desire to be so.

"I sat in his shadow," the lover sings, "and his fruit was sweet to my taste."

On a clear-skied evening in Asheville, a blue-eyed mountain man comes and sits next to me at a country bar near the river where I'm reading a book and sipping whiskey. "What are you reading?" he asks me, simple as can be. I smile and tell him. And later, as the sun sinks down, he fixes his blue eyes on mine and leans in to kiss me.

This is how you take a photograph of joy: stand just above the cloud line with a man you'll never see again but who made you tremble as the sun rose through the blue hills and the birds began to sound their first alarm. He's kinder to me than anyone has been in a long while, scraping up a batch of sausage and eggs in a cast-iron skillet as I sit on the steps and watch. Later that morning we sleep curled together in a heap, my head on his chest. In his truck on the way home I sit back with one foot on the dash and watch the meadows roll by as Rose, his dog, pants with her head out the window.

I have memorized this photograph. It is a picture of freedom after years of striving. I am wearing a shirt stolen from his closet, walking toward him as the sky behind me hurtles toward an afternoon thunderstorm. My head is cast to the side, caught mid-laugh. Rose looks up at me, panting, ready to run.

No one can tell me this isn't some kind of love. There are no bands on our fingers, no promises made, no need to call tomorrow or the next day. I don't know his last name, and I won't ever know it, and tomorrow he'll drive away and I won't see him or the dog named Rose again. Though two thousand years of church teachings imply that what we've done is wrong, I know in the deepest hollow of my gut, the place from which God so often speaks to me, that it is good.

I have this photograph, of a woman unburdened by fear or commitment, transcendent with joy. She has hastened to the mountain and touched the holiness of God.

Back home in Brooklyn, I find my revulsion toward dresses unchanged. My closet is stuffed with flared skirts and flowery prints. I liked them well enough. But now, when I hold them to my body in the mirror, they feel like costumes.

Every day I burrow through my closet to find something that doesn't have a ruffled sleeve. I usually end up in jeans and a fitted blazer. I find myself searching for men's shoes in smaller sizes on the Web, and order a pair of blue oxfords with bright laces. When they arrive, I take them straight out of the box and change into them. Standing up and looking in the mirror, I break into a smile. For the first time, maybe ever, everything feels exactly right.

The morning of the New York Pride Parade, I'm rummaging through my clothes again, this time looking for anything rainbow colored. I snag an apron my mom sent me from the kitchen—thick fabric with vertical rainbow stripes—and try to fold it into something awesome. In the end, I wear it backward over my clergy collar, like a cape, then bobby pin a handful of feathers in red, yellow, green, and blue into my short hair. A pair of tight jean shorts, red low-heeled cowboy boots, and a rainbow heart pinned to my chest like a Care Bear, and I am ready.

I stride down the block in this getup, giddy with excitement. This is the first time St. Lydia's has marched in the Pride Parade, and I can't wait. I still feel loose and free from my time on sabbatical. My joy goes unnoticed by my fellow passengers as I board the subway. New Yorkers have a miraculous, cultivated ability to sit next to a woman wearing a backward apron-turned-superhero Pride cape on the F train and never lift their eyes from Candy Crush.

Emerging from the subway near the New York Public Library, I revel in the chance to roam down the broad avenue, which has been blocked off from traffic. It feels strange and exciting to stride down the yellow lane markers with no fear of being hit. Everything is broken open. There is space that wasn't there before.

I find our little crew of fifteen or so congregants taking refuge in the shade. Alicia and her girlfriend, Liz, who organized us to march, are unrolling vinyl banners. Leah's wearing a very un-British cowboy hat and a rainbow feather boa. Hannah's there in a swirly skirt and sandals, and Omar is scantily clad and covered in glitter.

"I sooooo wish my old pastors could see this," Omar says to me, elated.

The Pride March in New York City is a strange irony. The first one took place in 1970, a year after the Stonewall riots. Up until then, the primary actor on the stage for gay rights was the Mattachine Society, which organized silent, dignified vigils. Seeking to be accepted by the dominant culture, they disallowed hand-holding or kissing, and required men to wear suits and lesbians to don skirts or dresses.

In 1970, it was against the law to "solicit men for the purpose of committing a crime against nature." You could lose your job if you were gay. You could get booted out of your apartment. You could get thrown in jail for "cross-dressing" or beat up by the cops. It was illegal for men to dance with other men. Gay bars were all underground, and the Stonewall was raided, all the time. Then, in June 1969, the street kids fought back.

A year later, gay people marched out in the open. Titled the Christopher Street Liberation March, this was a new kind of movement. After Stonewall, New York Queers weren't so interested in being respectable. They just wanted to be who they were. They carried plain card-board signs attached to mailing tubes that said, simply, "Gay Pride." There were no floats, balloons, or music. There was only the empty expanse of Sixth Avenue (the march had received a permit) and a line of cops with their backs turned.[4]

Today's march seems different, at least on the surface. Activists point out that what began as a protest march has turned into something more akin to a parade. Giant floats are poised waiting in the streets, sponsored by cellphone companies and vodka brands. And the cops who entrapped and roughed up Queer kids? The cops who turned a blind eye to the deaths of trans people and raided Stonewall? They now line the streets, waving. Getting arrested is still dangerous when you're trans or Black. But at this particular moment, under the summer sun, the cops are smiling, rainbow flags pinned to their lapels.

Our little band of churchgoers assembles on the pavement in front of a float for SAGE, an advocacy group for LGBTQ elders, who are perched high above us. They gaze down, wrapped in rainbow flags and waving hand fans to keep cool. They saw things we didn't see, fought fights so we won't have to.

There is what seems like an interminable wait in the shadow of the SAGE float, and then, at once, we are off. We march, the Empire State Building piercing the sky behind us. The streets are ours. Alongside the Lydians, I dance my way down Sixth Avenue. I ride the explosive energy of the crowd, cheering and waving their flags to the pulse of the music. We wave energetically toward the side-lines, a celebration of bodies, glistening with sweat and glitter in hot shorts.

What does it mean to live fully in your body, unfurling yourself like a banner, releasing your soul to flutter toward joy? In the book of Exodus, Moses stands before Pharaoh, who has enslaved his people, and demands their freedom. When the Israelites flee, God parts the sea and brings them safely through to the other side. There, a woman named Miriam takes up her tambourine and whirls and dances, skirt flying and feet pounding, head thrown back in full-throated joy.

You have to travel through deep waters to find your-self, finally, on the other side. Like Miriam, I don't know yet what freedom means. I've never lived in this land be-fore. But I know for sure that I am there now. I can taste it on my tongue and it's like sweet honey. On Sixth Ave-nue I find that I can't stop dancing. I've shed something that needed to go, and seen a glimpse of how to be whole. I don't understand it yet, but I know I am on the cusp of a delicious and explosive integration. I know that I can be a woman and a pastor, alive and free, unfettered and whole.

The word "Queer" has not yet crossed my tongue, and won't for a few years. But it's coming. Today a liberation that started decades ago has reached me through wordless ecstasy. It is the inhale before sound or speech, the moment before the rising of the sun. The dawn is here and the day is coming.

So I dance.

In March of the following year, I announce my departure from St. Lydia's. It's been a long discernment. A long time sifting through my own needs and the congregation's, my own call and questions about what should come next. I know that God is drawing me away. I pour out my heart in a letter to the congregation, edit it and fine-tune it over weeks. After hitting send, I sit in my apartment, stunned. Sunday night, a congregant takes me aside and says, "We're going to miss you. I wasn't expecting this—that you were going to leave. But when I read your letter I thought, *Yes, that makes sense. It feels right.*"

At the end of April we celebrate my final Easter Vigil with the people of St. Lydia's. Saturday night we light the new fire out on the sidewalk, then process inside, each holding a lit candle, and sit in the darkness of a still room. In that holy, quiet space, we tell the story of "salvation history," as it is called. After a year of hearing bits and pieces of stories from the Bible, fragments of poetry, song, and shreds of gospel, we sit back and start at the beginning. Omar tells the first story tonight: of how God created the heavens and the earth from nothingness, and brought light and life.

Charlotte tells the story of Noah and the ark, how the chaotic waters came and covered everything he knew, lapping at the boat until it was carried up and away into a new and unknown world, where a bow hung in the sky. She's made a great boat out of cardboard and given us all yards of blue fabric to wave up and down like the sea.

We tell the story of Jonah, who tries to run from God but is swallowed by a fish and brought to the bottom of the ocean, because that's what life feels like when you fight like hell to avoid your calling. Ezra and his two daughters tell that one, with a blue construction paper fish and the tiny figure of Jonah, and we all laugh big belly laughs.

We tell these stories of how God was with us at the beginning of creation, and how God brought us through: the Red Sea, the great flood, the belly of the fish, the dryness of bones, of the bread that is offered though we may have no money, and finally, of the teacher and healer and agitator God sent to be by our side, who would show that love is more powerful than death.

The story does not belong to me. It is held by these people, who stand around this table. I yearned to draw them together; now they are here.

In recent days, I have started crying in unexpected moments. Finishing up a batch of emails, I shed my clothes and jump in the shower, only to find myself overtaken by sobs. These crying jags come and find me, like wolves stalking prey. I cannot predict their arrival. Sometimes on the subway, holding a paperback open with one hand, tears will start streaming down my cheeks.

My body knew of my departure before I spoke it out loud. Years ago, when Rachel told me she was leaving St. Lydia's, she said it felt like a breakup. Now I know what she meant. Something is happening to me I'm not quite in control of. It is less a choice than a birth, and the sobs are contractions. I've learned that God doesn't only call us *to* places, God also calls us away. If I cling to this church, I'll end up like Jonah in the belly of a construction paper fish, at the bottom of the sea.

This Easter Saturday night, we dance with everything we have. We dance like Miriam crossing into the land of liberation. We dance because together we have tasted freedom.

"Christ is risen," I call to the congregation.

"He is risen indeed," the Lydians shout back to me. When we say it, remember it, shout it, we can affirm with our whole souls that death is not final, and that in the midst of all of it, we have found life. Julia flicks on the lights, and we sing our way to the table.

"Holy food for holy people," I say, and break the bread. We are holy not because we are good but because we are loved. We are loved not because we deserve it but because we are of God.

We raise our glasses and lean on one another's shoulders, dancing around the table in a whirl, the communion bread at the center. Baked into the bread are dyed Easter eggs, symbols of life contained but waiting to erupt. We get tipsy and laugh. We stomp our feet. We are a church.

I have told you this story. A story is different from the truth. The truth has rough edges and loose threads. The truth has days that are messy or boring, where nothing works and everything's wrong. I could tell you about the day when our payroll processing situation was so hopelessly muddled, I buried my head in my elbow and really thought I was going to cry while waiting on hold for customer service. But it wouldn't be a very good story.

I could tell you about the fight Rachel and I had that was so bad we thought everything might actually be broken beyond repair. But that fight is not the most important thing about who we were to each other.

This is not a perfect story and I was not a perfect pastor, and it's interesting that I wish I was, or wanted to be, because the whole point of St. Lydia's was to be not perfect, together. Did I miss my faults? Did I make myself better than I was? Are we too hard on ourselves, or too easy? What do we do with the distance between the two?

But stories are also the way we make sense of the world. They're the center of our sacred texts. Stories of things that Jesus said and did, people he touched and places he went that everyone remembers, but everyone remembers them just a bit differently.

Stories are not true. But stories are truth.

There is a story in the Gospel of Luke about two disciples who we've never met before. One of them is named Cleopas, and the other one never gets a name. These disciples are walking on a road, and as they walk, Jesus comes and walks with them. But they don't realize it's him. They think it's just a stranger. The stranger asks them questions about the unbelievable things that have happened in Jerusalem. The infamous teacher and prophet and rabble-rouser who was demonstrating in the temple and inciting violence among the people—he's been executed by the state, they tell him. But now these women from their group are saying that they saw him again and he's not really dead.

Jesus walks alongside the men, smiling to himself a little and listening as his friends spill out their story. They are in that stage where something so unreal and shocking has happened, and you can't understand it until you have told it over and over.

Cleopas and his nameless friend don't know this man walking alongside them, but there is something about him that feels sure and safe. Whoever he is, they need more of him, and they plead with him to share dinner with them. He does. There is a loaf of bread, and the stranger takes it and blesses it and breaks it, and in that instant they understand: this stranger is God and he is sitting beside them.

Then he is gone.

It's a story about transcendence. In Latin, *trans* means "across," and *scandere* means "to climb." Transcendence happens in moments when a boundary is crossed and we defy the limits that usually define our lives—when something sacred happens in an ordinary place. For these two men, transcendence comes when the stranger they met on the road blesses the bread and then breaks it. In an instant, they realize that their hearts have been burning. A boundary disintegrates, and they see things for what they are: God in the face of a stranger, sitting with them and sharing a meal.

But the thing about transcendent moments is they don't last for long. Christ vanishes, and we are left with only longing, and broken bread.

A remarkable amount of the Gospels takes place in the wake of trauma. Jesus meets and heals people whose lives have left them with few choices. People who can't escape their demons. Women who can't escape what everyone says about them. People who are so sick they've lost hope. People who are grieving after losing the person they love. Jesus meets these people in the midst of lives that are not what anyone would have hoped for. When he leaves, they don't have much to hold on to: just these few moments of transcendence when Jesus came and walked alongside them on the road and their hearts burned with longing.

"Stay with us," the disciples told him. And he did. Just for a moment, they caught a glimpse of God. It might not always feel like enough. But it's what we have.

My last service at St. Lydia's, we pack everyone into 304 Bond Street. Standing up to preach, I tell my congregants that I've found God in each of their faces, gathered around our tables, waiting and expectant for a small fragment of bread. Like all of us, I've experienced doubt and distance from God. "But you," I tell them, "gave me a rare gift: that of certainty." I have sat next to God at the table. She was there each time the bread was broken. I longed for connection. Look what I found.

I return to my seat as Charlotte stands to lead a song. Their faces lift toward her as she lines out each phrase for them to sing back. I wonder what difference our little church has made in their lives, and how it will continue to change them.

Ezra has made it through that terrible uncertain year of divorce. He's started dating, and he still brings his kids to church. Charlotte has launched her own theater troupe and is putting on a series of shows at St. Lydia's, crowdfunding them herself and storing her puppets in our basement. Phil and Wendy got married last spring, with me presiding. I invited the congregation to lay hands on them in a blessing, Peter between them, as a new family took shape. Hannah found courage to share her full self with the world, her true name, her call as an organizer, and some very cute dresses. Omar is starting art school.

Who would we be if we hadn't befriended Mr. Heyward and Tracey, if we hadn't worked alongside Onleilove? Who would we be if we had never seen Sydney's or Ethan's photograph? Would we have plunged buckets into the cold floodwaters of a stranger's basement in the wake of that terrible storm? Who would we be if we hadn't had one another to pray us along, or these tables to return to when we faltered?

After blessing the cup and doing the dishes, the people of St. Lydia's gather around and lay hands on me. I am made heavy with blessings and grace. They send me out as we have sent out so many others, and then the grace and blessing spill out the door and down the street to a bar where we laugh and dance and have a few drinks.

When there are just a few of us left, Hannah says, "Emily, can we see your van?"

I have purchased a rickety 1994 Dodge Ram van that the previous owner converted into a camper. There's a bed in the back and string lights hung across the windows. I am deep in research mode, deciding whether I should install a fridge or just buy a really good cooler. All my grief is poured into creating this small home on wheels that will carry me, I hope, across the country on an adventure that is, honestly, quite out of character. But it is the only thing I can do. I want to belong to no one for a while.

The van is parked around the corner, and we giggle out of the bar and down the street to find it. I fumble with the locks, pull back the sliding door, flip on the string lights, and we all pile in.

"Oh my gosh, this is so nineties," Omar says, investigating the wood laminate built-in storage.

Hannah says, "I feel like we should bless your van. Maybe sing a song?"

With her newfound voice she teaches us one. It's a new song—one we've never sung before.

Next Sunday night, I am gone. They break the bread without me.

Distant Seas

The cheapest way to travel to Alaska by ferry, and the most adventurous, I think, is to buy a walk-on ticket and pitch a tent on the ship's rear deck. This is a custom on the Alaska Marine Highway System, which departs near the Canadian border from a port in Bellingham, Washington, and sails for four days and three nights before reaching Juneau.

I'm headed north, farther north than I've ever been, to preside at the wedding of two dear friends. The last four weeks have been a winding journey: a tent pitched in the backwoods among puppeteers in Vermont; a sunny spare room at a friend's enormous Victorian when my van predictably ended up in the shop; then I parked the van in a friendly driveway in Boston and boarded a plane to Seattle to visit my parents; and now, this ferry.

My mom walks me over to the terminal. I'm wearing a backpack, and she's carrying my cooler. We enact a whole scene in the line for the foot passengers as she tries to take my picture—she doesn't know which button to push, and the phone keeps going back to the home screen. Soon we are both doubled over with laughter.

We attract the attention of all the old couples waiting to board. They are the sorts of people who wear fleece cardigans and white sneakers and have binoculars dangling around their necks. The women have let their hair grow out in shades of natural gray or white, swept back into a single, long braid. Aboard the ferry, they sit on the deck and point out passing ships, birds they've sighted. These couples seem easy with one another. Worn in.

I follow another woman traveling on her own to the top deck, and we both break out duct tape, pitching our tents and taping them down with long strips. We are both immediately hit on by a man in coveralls, and politely send him packing. I set out to wander the vessel.

For the next four days, I recede into my body like a snail in its shell. My mind grows small and quiet, and the world around me slows. I speak to almost no one. As we churn our way north, I stand at the bow of the boat, wrapped in a windbreaker and hat against the wind, or curl with a book in the window seat of a closed cocktail lounge with dated maritime décor. I take hot showers in the compact stalls of the women's locker room. I nap in corners of the various observation lounges, sample the cuisine in the cafeteria, and dash off the boat while stopped in Ketchikan to stock up on items at the A & P. I wonder about the pair of Franciscan friars in brown robes who have boarded together, setting up their tents on the deck alongside me. I complete eight rows of knitting and gasp when two orcas breach alongside the boat. We all gasp together. That they could be so close and so real and so wild!

The table gathers. But resurrection, it turns out, scatters. When the women find an empty tomb, cavernous and cold, they experience only fear and disorientation. The natural order of things—cells that multiply in a warm, dark place; blood that moves from birth to growth, and finally, one day, to illness and age, decay and decomposition—has been reversed. They've come to anoint his body in death, but instead the corpse is missing and an otherworldly ambassador informs them that the world has turned backward, the sun has reversed its course.

The disciples, too, find themselves confused and fractured in the wake of their friend's execution. In the posttraumatic haze, they fish but catch nothing. They glimpse his face in a crowd, and their hearts stop, but it's only someone who looks like him. They dream he is close, the heat of his body just behind them, so close they can feel it, his breath or his voice. They awaken and he is gone. They fish all night, hoping to find him because they are lost.

Then, look: he is there. He tells them to cast the net on the other side, and there are fish, too many to know what to do with, and a warm fire on the beach. He is there eating, alive but also wounded, gone but present at the same time.

What does it mean that God comes so close to dwell with us and then goes away, leaving us to struggle along on our own? What are we to make of her ephemeral arrivals, which seem impossibly tied to her unending presence? Can we live with a God who is here and yet gone? Who gives everything for us and then vanishes?

Jesus gathered people around tables, but he also sent them out on roads. For every meal he shared, every drawing together around a heavy-laden table, there was a call to travel an unknown path. He sends us to figure it out as we go, teaching or healing or starting churches or just muddling through. Along the way, though, there are tables.

I have been scattered; this is my road. The disciples followed their grief to the water, and I do too, letting out my net again and again, hoping I might pull up something, some fragment of who I am, a memory of my ancestors who lived in this region, a way through the memory of their sin, and mine. When I was little my mom stuffed my chubby arms through the sleeves of the baptismal gown that belonged to my grandmother, and the pastor held me in her arms and scooped water from the font.

"Emily, I baptize you in the name of the Father, and of the Son, and of the Holy Spirit," she said, and I let out a cry. With well-worn words, she promised me that I was a child of God, and no matter how far I wandered, God would always find me. Even if I traveled to the ends of the earth, or left myself behind, or lost the people who loved me, or sank down, down, down, to the bottom of the sea.

The last night of the journey, I sleep on a deck chair in the open air. The mountains are all cool blues and white, and I make myself a hot chocolate from the cafeteria's industrial water heater before heading to the deck. I settle into my chair and nestle in my sleeping bag, the mountains receding as we head north, and north and north.

There's a group of high school kids in the tents next to me—sweet teenagers in outdoor gear who've come here on a school trip. One of the girls told me about it in the women's room as we all brushed our teeth.

"It's a course on the ecology of south Alaska," she said, a baseball hat holding her hijab in place, "but we drove all the way from Omaha in a fifteen-passenger bus, and we're just . . . kind of tired." I agreed that it was a whole lot of transport, and wished them well.

Tonight on the deck, four of the girls are teaching each other a line dance. There's no reception and no Wi-Fi on this ship; without their devices, the students have regressed to the year 1860, clasping hands with their partners and swinging them round. The leader somehow cajoles the whole group up and arranges them in two circles.

"Right right right, left left left," they chant before do-si-doing. Behind me one of the Franciscans, wearing a windbreaker over his brown habit, smiles and nods. The girls are lovely, laughing as they twirl. Beneath them the engine of the boat roars.

The ferry plunges forward through a darkening passageway of ever-erupting peaks. Their beauty is dangerous and insistent. We have sailed through the Strait of Georgia. My great-grandfather's ashes are scattered there. My great-grandmother Beatrice's life was lost to these seas. We sail north, the engines pushing me along through waves of grief and unknowing, past the edges of my sense of self.

I have left my apartment, my city, my friends, my church. I have left my Lydians. Who am I if they are not there to tell me? If they aren't there to show me the way to the deepest version of myself: that person who, despite my rough edges and sharp corners, is loved? Who am I if I am not holding a loaf of bread in my hands?

Is tonight Sunday? I wonder. Are they gathered around the tables? Is someone reading from our sacred book?

"Please share a word or phrase that struck you in the text," I used to ask them after the reading.

Mountain. In my mind I hear an echo of Charlotte voicing a word from the story of an unnamed woman who goes to draw water and finds Jesus instead.

Ancestor, someone offers.

The well is deep.

The girls spin and dance and throw their heads back with laughter, spiraling together. The light becomes pale and

unearthly as the sun sinks down behind the ancient mountains; I have never been this far north before.

This is the memory I can't stop thinking about:

Trudging over to the Hoyt-Schermerhorn station with
a novel tucked in my bag and boarding the A train. Finding a corner seat away from the doors and opening my
book. It's a few weeks before my departure, and I'm headed
to the last stop.

I've dreaded this moment for months. Telling Ula is
the very worst part of leaving.

Lutherans focus not on the person of the pastor but on
the office. There will be a pastor after me to love Ula. The
congregation will keep loving her in my absence. But
today none of that seems to matter. I feel like I am aban-
doning her, and I don't want to. All these years of building
this church, she's always been here.

The last year has been a tough run for Ula. She was set
to transfer to a better rehabilitation facility, then became
ill during the transfer and landed in the hospital. Her personal items were scattered between Brooklyn and Queens
and then sent to a new nursing home in Crown Heights,
where she became, suddenly, extremely despondent. On
visiting, I'd find her sitting in a chair in the common area,
unwilling or unable to speak with me. Then she was back
in the hospital, where her behavior became completely er-
ratic.

"She's not usually like this," I told the nurses. "She's
smart and she makes sense when she talks."

"Oh . . ." they said. "So this is different from her base-line?"

Finally the doctors uncovered the cause of her dementia-like symptoms. With treatment, she began to return to herself. But she'd lost her place at the better re-habilitation facility, so they transferred her to a nursing home near Far Rockaway. The last stop on the A train.

Far Rockaway is called that because it is far. Far from everything. Past the airport, an hour-and-a-half train ride from Manhattan. It was too far for a Lydian to go and help Ula get to church. The trip would have taken three hours, and that's if the Access-A-Ride was on time.

Ula was always striving. Always pushing toward a life beyond her capacity. From a wheelchair in the Rockaways she'd tell me that she wanted to finish the degree she had started at New York Theological Seminary. By that point, she couldn't really read, and her only income came from social security checks. But still she was focused on getting there.

After her stroke she was sweet but panicked, so rarely in control of what was happening to her—her meals, her schedule, her ability to make choices and move independently. She was always the casual subject of someone's sentence, always a slip of paperwork in a pile.

Once, I watched her go to pieces when the nurses at the home asked us to sort through the garbage bags of stuff she had arrived with. Bewildered, she would pick up one crumpled paper at a time, a bottle of unopened soda, and declare that she needed it all.

"She's been dispossessed too many times," an old friend of hers told me.

The train pulls into the elevated station. It's still cold outside, with a stiff ocean breeze, but as I walk under the tracks, there are small blue flowers blooming along the sidewalk.

ID tag on my chest, I head up to Ula's room and knock tentatively at the door. We chat for a while, but I'm barely suppressing my anxiety, and keep taking deep breaths. I help her with her new cellphone. The touch pad is harder for her to manipulate than the old-fashioned flip phone, which had buttons she could feel.

Ula wants to go outside, so I push her down the hall to the elevator and down another hallway. We line up with a procession of elderly men in wheelchairs or on crutches for the home's officially sanctioned smoke break. Incredibly, a nurse appears with a Tupperware box full of cigarettes, opens the door to the roof area, and doles out the smokes one at a time to the waiting men. I guess they're only allowed one a day, and this is their chance. She even has a selection of brands. Ula and I pass on the cigarettes, and I push her out into the fresh air.

"So, Ula," I begin, "I have some news." I feel like a traitor and a sellout.

When I tell her, I start crying.

"Oh," she says, head nodding up and down in understanding, her damaged hand gripping the armrest of her wheelchair. "It's okay, it's okay."

"Ula!" I say. "I'm supposed to be comforting you, not the other way around."

"You have to go and do what's in front of you," she says simply.

"I know," I mumble, weeping. "I'm so sorry."

All these years in New York, I've been looking for something. Trying to find some wholeness or resolution that I thought a relationship might bring. Trying to reach the end of loneliness. I didn't find love, but I found Ula.

The two of us sit together, her in her wheelchair, me on a metal folding chair. I bring my tears under control and ask her questions—anything I can think of—which she answers in her halting way. She complains about the patient in the next room over who plays her television too loud, and tells me that she's not getting enough physical therapy.

"Well, let's go visit the nursing office on the way back to your room and we can ask about it," I say, putting my hand on her shoulder. We look out over the concrete wall, the oversized exhaust fan humming loudly next to us.

"Ula, look," I say. "If you sit up really straight, you can see the ocean." I have this desire to give her something beautiful, something she can keep.

She props herself up on the arms of her wheelchair, stretching up, reaching forward. We crane our necks together. And through the chain-link fence, beyond the storm-battered apartment buildings, past the elevated train tracks and the tangle of humanity and hope and loss, we can just catch sight of the blue of the sea.

ACKNOWLEDGMENTS

A book isn't written alone. I am grateful for the community of people who helped make this one real.

There would be no story without the people of St. Lydia's. Each one of you is a part of this book's pages. St. Lydia's would never have been without the partnership of Rachel Pollak Kroh. Thank you for every woodcut, email salutation, lock-shaped candle, and dishcloth banner. In addition, St. Lydia's was shaped by each staff person and intern gutsy enough to take a risk on a wobbly new start: Julia Macy Offinger, Hannah Johnston, Sarah McCaslin, Rebecca Stevens-Walter, Zachary Stevens-Walter, Joel Avery, Alissa Kretzmann Farrar, Jack Holloway, and Melissa O'Keefe Reed.

Tim Kreider showed me that I'm a writer and taught me along the way. Thank you for talking me down all those times I was spazzing. Jacob Slichter read an early, clunky draft and told me what this book was actually about. Thank you for your faith: in me, in communities, and in the faltering church. Burke Gerstenschlager walked me through the drafting, pitching, and publication process with tireless enthusiasm. Thank you for being my dial-a-friend for all questions theological and mythological.

I am endlessly grateful to Derek Reed, my kind, patient, and thoughtful editor, as well as the entire team at Convergent. I am particularly thankful for David Kopp, who saw early on that I had a story to tell and encouraged me.

Meg Thompson, my literary agent, really is some kind of magic.

I am surrounded by friends and coconspirators who support me and my work fiercely. This book would not exist without the love and friendship of Nadia Bolz-Weber and Rachel Held Evans. I am heartbroken that Rachel cannot see the growing body of work her advocacy made possible.

Nancy McLaren, Mieke Vandersall, Jeff Chu, Lenny Duncan, and Ever Hanna all read drafts and told me the truth.

Kerlin Richter, Austin Channing Brown, Jes Kast, Neichelle Guidry, Rozella Haydée White, Jodi Houge, Mihee Kim Kort, Nichole Flores, Rachel Kurtz, and Winnie Varghese sustained me along the way.

Donald Schell, Phil Trzynka, and Daniel Simons walked at my side through the founding of St. Lydia's and along my winding path toward serving as a pastor. No words can capture my gratitude for their love and guidance.

I was honored to write about leaders in the Gowanus

Community and grateful to each for trusting me with a part of their story. Tracey Pinkard collaborated with me and St. Lydia's with an open heart, shared her perspectives, and reviewed the "Good Fridays" chapter. Ms. Donna Heyward graciously allowed me to share the story of Nicholas Naquan Heyward, Jr., and Mr. Nicholas Heyward, who passed away in January 2019. Mr. Heyward taught me, and many others, what tireless dedication to justice looks like.

Onleilove Alston taught me immeasurably, and reviewed the "Empty Tombs" chapter. Thank you to the team at Faith in New York, as well as Shatia Strother and Michael Higgins at Families United for Racial and Economic Equality, gifted organizers who bring the world as it should be a little closer.

Hannah Soldner, Charlotte Moroz, Omar Abreu, Phil Fox Rose, Wendy Barrie, and Ula Barrack allowed me to share a small piece of their stories. Liz Edman coordinated St. Lydia's participation in the Pride Parade and suggested the David Kirby photograph for our Good Friday liturgy. Andrew Lipsett consulted with me on the "Good Fridays" chapter in regard to redlining practices and discrimination in Memphis, Tennessee. Jeff Stark graciously reviewed the "Lost Things" chapter.

St. Lydia's is supported by the Metropolitan New York Synod and the Evangelical Lutheran Church in America. Grant funding, piles of paperwork, and fervent prayers were all needed to bring something from nothing. Thank you for taking a risk on us.

I wrote this book all over the nation, in guest rooms,

borrowed chalets in the mountains, and a camper van named Edith Van Trundle (may she rest in peace). Thank you to Holden Village, Chris Craun, Lauren Muratore, Diana Carroll and Sarah Lamming, and Christo Allegra (who let me far outstay my welcome when my van was in the shop).

Atticus Zavaletta, thank you for loving this book as well as you love me. You are, impossibly, both the end and the beginning of my story.

NOTES

Prologue

1. Jane Kenyon, "Briefly It Enters, and Briefly Speaks," in *Collected Poems* (St. Paul: Greywolf Press, 2005).

I. Creation

1. *New Interpreter's Bible*, vol. 10 (Nashville: Abingdon Press, 2002), 231–232.
2. Kyna Leski, *The Storm of Creativity* (Cambridge, Mass.: MIT Press, 2015).

II. Enough

1. *The Dreary Coast*, written and directed by Jeff Stark in 2014, was an immersive theatrical work. The work explored the character and perspective of Charon, the ferryman of the underworld, and leaned on and reinterpreted Greek myth, in particular, the stories of Persephone, Hades, and the "descent" themes found in the stories of Orpheus and Eurydice. An imaginative retelling of ancient stories, *The Dreary Coast*

wove together characters and themes from such diverse ancient sources as Hesiod, Homer, and Ovid.

2. Joseph Alexiou, *Gowanus: Brooklyn's Curious Canal* (New York: New York University Press, 2015).
3. Alexiou, *Gowanus: Brooklyn's Curious Canal.*
4. Alexiou, *Gowanus: Brooklyn's Curious Canal.*

III. Justice

1. With thanks to Lenny Duncan, who consulted with me on this chapter. Lenny Duncan, personal communication, July 2019.
2. For more on redlining see Richard Rothstein's *The Color of Law* (New York: Liveright Publishing Corporation, 2017).
3. Lenny Duncan, personal communication, July 2019.
4. Evan Osnos, "Doomsday Prep for the Super-Rich," *The New Yorker,* January 22, 2017.
5. Osnos, "Doomsday Prep for the Super-Rich."
6. In the opening paragraph of his book, *Rules for Radicals,* Saul Alinsky writes, "What follows is for those who want to change the world from what it is to what they believe it should be." Dependent on the Jewish belief of Olam HaBa, or "the world to come," this phrase not only reflects a Jewish understanding of the afterlife, a time after the arrival of the Messiah, but has become a commonly used framework for organizers of many faiths and no faith.

IV. Resurrection

1. J. Cheryl Exum, "Song of Songs," in *Women's Bible Commentary* (Louisville: Westminster John Knox Press, 2012), 249.

2. Exum, "Song of Songs," 249.

3. David M. Carr, *The Erotic Word: Sexuality, Spirituality, and the Bible* (Oxford: Oxford University Press, 2003), 119.

4. Fred Sargant, "1970: A First-Person Account of the First Gay Pride March," *The Village Voice*, June 22, 2010, https://www.villagevoice.com/2010/06/22/1970-a-first-person-account-of-the-first-gay-pride-march/.

ABOUT THE AUTHOR

EMILY M. D. SCOTT founded St. Lydia's Dinner Church, a progressive, LGBTQ+-affirming congregation in Brooklyn, New York, where worship takes place around the dinner table. A Lutheran pastor (ELCA), Scott is a graduate of Yale Divinity School and the Institute of Sacred Music. Her writing has appeared in *The New York Times*, and her work at St. Lydia's, which sparked a wider Dinner Church movement, has been featured in *The Wall Street Journal* and *The Atlantic*. After serving eight years at St. Lydia's, Scott is now creating a new church community, Dreams and Visions, in Baltimore, Maryland.

ABOUT THE TYPE

This book was set in Caslon, a typeface first designed in 1722 by William Caslon (1692–1766). Its
widespread use by most English printers in the
early eighteenth century soon supplanted the Dutch
typefaces that had formerly prevailed. The roman is
considered a "workhorse" typeface due to its pleasant, open appearance, while the italic is exceedingly
decorative.